You
Will Forever
Regret
Not Having Read
This Book

You Will Forever Regret Not Having Read This Book

by Flobse Wild

You Will Forever Regret Not Having Read This Book

First published on Amazon, 2025

ISBN: 9798287594176

Imprint: Independently published

In case of questions, remarks, or media requests, please visit:

www.flobsewild.com

www.youwillforeverregret.com

Or email us at: contact@flobsewild.com

For her,

You probably don't realize this,
but you inspired this book.
You called me "cool" and "interesting" - and that second word stayed
with me.
When things didn't work out between us,
I decided to become someone even more interesting -
to understand myself, the world, and everything in between.
This book is part of that journey.
Thank you.

Disclaimer

This book is written to the best of the author's knowledge, understanding, and experience. While every effort has been made to ensure the accuracy of the information presented, the content is not intended as professional advice - medical, legal, scientific, or otherwise.

Readers are encouraged to think critically, explore topics further, and consult qualified experts where necessary. The author and publisher disclaim liability for any actions taken based on the contents of this book.

This book is a reflection of learning, curiosity, and the human drive to understand the world - not a substitute for personal judgment or professional consultation.

Copyright Notice

Table of Contents

Prologue

Why I wrote this book?

I like to ask why.

When we're kids, we ask questions constantly. Studies show that young children - especially around age 4 - can ask anywhere from 100 to 300 questions a day. One study from the U.K. found that kids ask an average of 73 questions per day, with some asking over 300. [1] "Why is the sky blue?", "Where does the sun go at night?", "What happens if I eat this bug?" Curiosity is their default setting.

But something strange happens as we grow up: we stop asking.

By adulthood, we ask far fewer questions - often fewer than 20 a day, and most of them are transactional: "Did you send the email?" or "What time is the meeting?" We stop asking out of wonder. We stop asking to understand the world.

Researchers suggest this decline begins around age five, just as formal education starts. In classrooms, children may ask just one or two questions per hour, while teachers ask hundreds. [2] Over time, the system subtly trains us to answer, not to wonder. We stop questioning - not because we lose interest, but because we've learned not to.

That's why I sometimes try to think like a 7-year-old again.

But that's just a side note.

The real reason I wrote this book is because - as far as I know - there's nothing else out there that explains how life actually works in a way that's simple, relatable, and meant for the average person. We've got textbooks for experts and TED Talks for specialists, but nothing that brings it all together: science, body, brain, society, and self.

I believe everyone deserves to understand how the world works.
How you work.
How the invisible systems around you connect and interact.

So this book is a journey - a guide that uses stories, analogies, metaphors, and curiosity to make science and life click. Because we don't learn best through jargon or formulas. We learn best when we can see it - in our heads. We learn through pictures.

I still remember a presentation my former boss gave, where he said our team was like a tree - our roots strong, our branches spreading as we learned more. I'll never forget that image. But I couldn't tell you what else he talked about that day.

That's the power of metaphor. That's how we remember.

And that's what I want this book to be:
A book full of things you'll never forget - not because they're complex, but because they finally make sense.

Let's begin.

Chapter 1: At Home

Before we begin, a question:

Why is it 7:00 a.m.?

Not just because your clock says so. But because the concept of time - minutes, hours, even seconds - is something humans invented, based on patterns in nature and refined by science.

We measure a second today not by the sun, but by atomic vibrations.

1 second = 9,192,631,770 vibrations of a cesium-133 atom.

This ultra-precise definition is set by the International System of Units and maintained globally by scientific organizations like the BIPM (International Bureau of Weights and Measures).

Thanks to these atomic standards, your GPS, phone, and digital life all sync perfectly - down to the nanosecond.

And here's where Einstein comes in.

In 1905, he revealed that time isn't fixed. It slows down the closer you are to massive objects (like Earth), and the faster you move through space. This is relativity.

It's not just theory - GPS satellites orbiting Earth tick slightly faster than clocks on the ground because of weaker gravity up there. Engineers have to adjust for this difference, or your location would be off by kilometers.

So when your alarm goes off at 7:00 a.m., it's not just time - it's relativity-adjusted time, confirmed by the vibration of atoms, flying through satellites, grounded in physics.

It's Saturday, 7:00 a.m.

You're lying in bed. Still. Half-asleep. The mattress under your back feels soft, solid, supportive. But what you're actually resting on isn't soft or solid at all.

It's atoms.

Everything around you - the bed, the blanket, the pillow, the air, your own body - is made of atoms. These are incredibly tiny particles, each one about a million times smaller than a grain of sand. And yet, they're arranged in such a way that they can hold your full body weight without collapsing.

Why don't you fall through your bed?

Because of electromagnetic repulsion. The outer parts of atoms are surrounded by electrons - tiny, negatively charged particles. When the atoms in your body come close to the atoms in your bed, the electrons in both start pushing against each other.

You never actually touch anything. Atoms just get really, really close - and push back. What you feel as "pressure" or "support" is actually the force between the electrons in your skin and the electrons in the mattress surface.

That's what's holding you up right now.

And while you slept, your body kept working.

Even though you were unconscious, your brain cycled through four sleep stages - light sleep, deep sleep, REM sleep, and back again. Your cells were cleaning up damaged proteins, processing memories, and repairing tissue. This process normally takes at least seven hours - that's why it's so important to get enough sleep. If you had cheese before bed, chances are your digestive system was busy, too - quietly breaking down fats and proteins while your brain fired up dream simulations in REM sleep.

Now you're awake. Thirsty.

That's normal. The human body loses about 300–500 milliliters of water overnight through breathing and skin evaporation. You didn't notice, but you were exhaling warm, moist air for 6–8 hours. That water needs to be replaced.

So you get up.

But even standing requires science.

The reason your feet don't float into the ceiling is gravity - the Earth's invisible pull on your body. That gravitational acceleration, about 9.81 m/s^2, means you need to exert force just to rise from bed. Your muscles use energy stored as ATP (adenosine triphosphate) to overcome that force and lift you up.

You walk to the kitchen. Every step uses a coordinated system of bones, muscles, nerves, and balance signals from your inner ear. You don't think about it - but your body is running hundreds of processes simultaneously.

You reach for a glass of water.

The glass itself is a marvel of chemistry. It started as sand (mostly silicon dioxide), which was heated to extreme temperatures until it melted, then cooled quickly to become solid again. Unlike metal or plastic, glass doesn't react chemically with water - which is why it doesn't change the taste.

Water - H_2O - is another miracle. Two hydrogen atoms bonded to one oxygen atom. It's a universal solvent, meaning it dissolves and carries nutrients inside your body. Your blood is about 50–60% water. Your brain? About 75% water. Your kidneys use water to filter waste. Your digestive system needs water to break down food.

Everything in your body needs water to function.

One of the most incredible things about the human body is how much of it runs without our permission.

You don't think about your kidneys - but they're constantly filtering your blood, removing toxins, balancing your electrolytes, and regulating your blood pressure. You don't think about your stomach - but it's digesting food using enzymes, acids, and muscle contractions in a perfectly timed sequence.

Your heart beats. Your lungs breathe. Your liver breaks down chemicals. Your pancreas regulates insulin.

All of this happens automatically, beneath your awareness. Your body is operating on a kind of biological autopilot - what we call the autonomic nervous system.

Now imagine this:

What if you had to control every heartbeat manually? What if you had to consciously tell your kidneys to start filtering, your stomach to digest, your liver to neutralize toxins - every second, without fail?

You wouldn't last 10 minutes.

The truth is, your subconscious mind and your body's internal systems are working together in a beautifully complex dance - one that most of us ignore entirely.

And yet, understanding even a little bit of how that system works can give you a whole new appreciation for yourself - and for life.

Inside all those water-filled cells is something even more fascinating: DNA.

Your DNA is a code - a long molecule made up of just four chemical bases (A, T, G, C) repeated in countless combinations. That code tells your body how to build proteins, how to grow, how to fight infection, how tall you are, even how you handle coffee.

Half of your DNA came from your mother. Half from your father. But it's not a perfect 50/50 split. Your DNA is also shaped by your grandparents, and their parents - passed through generations, like a biological relay race. And depending on your environment, some genes can switch on or off. This is called epigenetics.

Men have one X and one Y chromosome. Women have two X chromosomes. Just one difference - and yet an entire biological cascade comes from that small change in your chromosome setup.

And yet, despite all that complexity, you wake up every morning - mostly unaware of the incredible physics, chemistry, and biology that are keeping you alive.

But what if you didn't ignore it?

What if you understood it?

Let's continue.

You've had your water - ideally around 500 milliliters, to help rehydrate your body after a night of water loss through breathing and sweating. Now, it's time for fuel.

Your body needs energy to function - and it gets that energy from food. Everything you eat is made of molecules: fats, proteins, carbohydrates, vitamins, and minerals. When you eat, your digestive system breaks down those molecules and extracts chemical energy, primarily in the form of calories.

A calorie is a unit of energy. Technically, it's the amount of heat needed to raise the temperature of one gram of water by one degree Celsius. But in nutrition, we usually refer to kilocalories (kcal) - the energy your body gets from food to power your muscles, organs, brain, and more.

The number of calories you need depends on:

- Your body weight (and your goal: lose, maintain, or gain)

- Your activity level (sitting all day vs. running marathons)

- Your metabolism (how efficiently your body burns energy)

Without food, your body doesn't have the fuel to perform daily tasks - walking, thinking, healing, even breathing. You don't just eat for taste; you eat to stay alive, to regenerate, to move.

It's also important to understand how adaptable the human body is.

When you exercise regularly, your body becomes more efficient. Over time, it may adjust your metabolism - how quickly or slowly you burn energy - to better match your activity level. This adaptability is part of what makes humans so resilient.

In some extreme cases, especially in female athletes or individuals with very low body fat and high physical stress, the body may temporarily stop the menstrual cycle. This is called amenorrhea, and it's the body's way of prioritizing survival. If the body senses there's not enough energy to support a potential pregnancy, it may pause reproduction until conditions are more stable.

Menstruation itself is completely natural - and it should not be a taboo topic. It's a regular process, typically occurring once a month, where the uterus sheds its lining when a pregnancy does not occur. That lining, rich in blood and nutrients, exits the body through the vagina. This cycle prepares the body for a potential pregnancy and is a crucial sign of hormonal health.

In other words, your biology is constantly adapting - balancing energy, hormones, and survival priorities in real time. And that's incredibly intelligent.

Back to breakfast. As you lift your coffee cup - maybe with a bowl of cereal if you're trying to eat healthy - you carry it over to the kitchen table. You're holding it because, if you didn't, gravity would pull it straight to the ground.

As you walk to your chair and sit down, your body is constantly applying force. To carry the cup and food, you're using muscles to overcome gravity - a direct application of Newton's laws of motion. The more mass something has, the more force it requires to move. In this case, it's not much - just a lightweight cup and bowl - but the principle still applies. You begin to eat - hopefully slowly. As you chew, your teeth break down the food into smaller pieces while saliva mixes in, starting digestion right in your mouth.

Then you swallow - and the food travels down your esophagus, a muscular tube that connects your throat to your stomach. This happens through peristalsis - wave-like muscle contractions that gently push food downward, like squeezing toothpaste from a tube.

Once in your stomach, the food is churned and mixed with acid and enzymes. Think of it like a fruit press: nutrients are squeezed out for your body to absorb, while the rest moves on as waste.

From the stomach, food enters your small intestine, where most of the nutrient absorption happens. And here's something important - the food you eat doesn't act alone. Different nutrients interact with each other, sometimes helping and sometimes blocking absorption. For example, drinking coffee or tea right before or after a meal can reduce how much iron your body absorbs, especially from plant-based sources. On the other hand, vitamin C can increase iron absorption - which is why orange juice is often paired with iron-rich meals.

It takes only 6–10 seconds for food to reach your stomach, but the entire digestive process can take 24 to 72 hours, depending on what you've eaten. Carbs digest quickly; fats and proteins take longer. But on average, your breakfast stays in your body about one day.

When you're done eating, you move again - using kinetic energy to carry your dishes to the sink or dishwasher.

And here's the crazy part:

The comforts we take for granted each morning - running water, warm beds, sturdy walls - are relatively new. For most of human history, people moved from place to place, slept under stars, or built temporary shelters. The concept of a private, stable home only became common in the last 200 years or so, depending on where you live.

Your morning routine - your home itself - is a marvel of science, biology, and history.
And you haven't even left the house yet.

Chapter 2: At Work

It's Monday, 8:00 a.m.

You've just finished breakfast - maybe still in your underwear. Now it's time to get dressed. You pull on clothes made of cotton or polyester - materials likely produced in factories thousands of kilometers away. The fabric may have been spun in India, dyed in Bangladesh, and stitched in Vietnam, before being shipped across oceans to land in your local store... or to your doorstep after one click online.

The shirt you wear to work isn't just fabric - it's a story of global collaboration. The raw materials were harvested or synthesized. The fibers were spun, dyed (often with industrial chemicals), shaped, and sewn into garments. In some countries, outdated practices still persist - in rare cases, even lead-based dyes are used despite known health risks.

The logo on your chest? That was printed by an industrial machine - which itself was built by another company, using parts sourced from yet another. The economy is not a chain - it's a web. Interconnected. Layered. Invisible, but very real.

And all of that... just to get dressed.

Toxic Threads - Is There Lead in Your Clothing?

Lead and other heavy metals (like cadmium and chromium) are still occasionally found in clothing, especially in:

- Brightly dyed items, particularly reds, yellows, and greens.

- Inexpensive accessories (belts, bags, costume jewelry).

- Unregulated imports or fast-fashion items with unclear sourcing.

Recent Findings:

- In 2022, Canadian researchers found lead levels up to 20× above safe limits in garments from some fast-fashion retailers like Shein. [1]

- In the U.S., tests on products from discount stores revealed lead in over 25% of accessories - some up to 1.7% lead content. [2]

What You Can Do:

- Wash new clothes before wearing them - this removes some surface chemicals.

- Look for certifications like:

  - Oeko-Tex® Standard 100

  - GOTS (Global Organic Textile Standard)

  - Bluesign®

- Be cautious with extremely bright colors or non-certified brands, especially if they're very cheap.

It's not paranoia - it's just paying attention to the chemistry in your closet.

Once you're dressed for the day - hopefully slightly overdressed, and most importantly comfortable - you're already influencing your psychology. When you feel good in your clothes, you tend to feel more confident in yourself. That's not vanity - it's human nature.

Imagine showing up to a wedding in just a T-shirt. You'd probably feel underdressed, maybe even self-conscious. And that discomfort would show in your posture, your mood, even your conversations. The science of confidence often starts with what we wear - and how it makes us feel.

Now, fully dressed and ready, you walk toward your vehicle - maybe a car, maybe a scooter, maybe an electric bike. Whether it's powered by gasoline, electricity, or even hydrogen, it's a rolling bundle of engineering.

You open the door and sit down. The seat beneath you is probably made from synthetic materials - polyester, foam, maybe a blend with cotton. You're surrounded by metal, electronics, and fabrics. It feels clean inside, almost "empty" - but just like at home, you're still surrounded by atoms. You don't see them, but they're everywhere. You're made of them. So is your car.

The body of most cars - the chassis - is made of aluminum or steel. Steel is heavier but stronger; aluminum is lighter but less rigid. And somewhere beneath you is a reinforced T-beam structure, which you can't see but may save your life in an accident. It absorbs impact and stabilizes the frame.

But what makes all of this move is the engine - the heart of the car.

How Does a Car Engine Work?

In a Combustion Engine:

The fuel you pump into your tank contains chemical energy. According to the law of conservation of energy, energy can't be created or destroyed - only transformed.

Here's how that happens:

1. Fuel and air are injected into cylinders.

2. The piston compresses the mixture, increasing pressure.

3. A spark plug ignites it (no lighter needed!), causing a small, controlled explosion.

4. This explosion pushes the piston down, turning the crankshaft.

5. That motion is converted into kinetic energy - the force that spins your wheels.

Engines with more cylinders (like V6, V8, or V12) can produce more power - because more fuel is ignited and more pistons are pushing.

And when you brake? You're doing physics again: pressing the pedal transforms kinetic energy into heat through friction. The laws of motion and energy conversion are literally keeping you safe.

Ever wonder why sitting in a car going 120 km/h doesn't feel any different than sitting still?

Because your body doesn't feel speed.
It feels acceleration - a change in speed or direction.

When you're cruising at a constant velocity - whether 30 or 300 km/h - everything around you is moving at the same rate. You, the air in the cabin, the coffee in your cup - all are moving together, smoothly.

That's why it feels calm - even though you're covering the length of a football field every second.

But the moment you brake, accelerate, or turn - that's when your body reacts. That's acceleration.
Your inner ear (specifically, your vestibular system) detects these changes and signals your brain. That's why roller coasters feel intense - they rapidly change direction and speed.

In physics, this is explained by inertia - an object in motion stays in motion, unless acted on by a force. If everything is moving together in harmony, there's no perceived force. No tension. No feeling of motion.

It's only when that harmony breaks - when you stop suddenly, take a turn, or hit turbulence - that your body notices.

So next time you're flying in a jet or cruising on the highway, remember:
You're not sitting still.
You're gliding through space at incredible speed - and your body doesn't even notice.
Not because nothing's happening... but because everything's happening smoothly.

In Electric Cars:

Electric cars don't burn fuel - they run on stored electricity.

That energy lives inside a lithium-ion battery, which you recharge after a certain mileage.

So what happens in there?

- When you charge your car, electrons flow into the battery and are stored using chemical reactions.

- When you drive, those electrons flow back out - creating an electric current that powers the motor.

No explosions. No smoke. Just quiet energy transfer from chemistry to motion.

Thanks to your car - with its thousands of components and layers of safety features - you're moving through the world protected by both hardware and software. And software is becoming more important every year.

Sometimes, I wonder:
Why do we still have accidents?
With all the sensors and smart systems modern vehicles have, you'd
think they'd be impossible.

Here's how it works:

Sensors in your car - like ultrasonic, radar, or lidar sensors - constantly
scan the environment around you. Some detect distances by sending out
waves or photons, and when those bounce back, the system calculates
how far away objects are. If something's too close (like another car or a
wall), the system sends a signal to warn you, or in advanced models, the
car might automatically brake.

Sensors don't always require traditional electricity to function at the
sensing point - some work on passive reflection of light or radio waves.
But the signal processing behind them still relies on electrical circuits
and software algorithms.

This blend of physics, hardware, and digital intelligence is what allows
autonomous features to exist at all.

So next time your car beeps as you reverse or even stops for you at the
last second - that's not magic.
That's photons, electrons, and math... all working to keep you safe.

Of course, not every workday starts with a car or scooter.
Sometimes, your job - or your break from it - requires a plane.

Whether it's a quick business trip or a long-overdue vacation, stepping
onto a plane is stepping into one of humanity's greatest technological
feats.
But how do planes actually fly?

At first, it feels impossible: a giant metal tube, heavier than your house,
rising into the sky and staying there.

It's not magic. It's physics.
Specifically, a beautiful balance of forces.

The wings of a plane are specially shaped - the top is curved, the bottom flatter. This design is called an airfoil. As the plane moves forward, air flows faster over the curved top and slower beneath. According to Bernoulli's Principle, faster-moving air means lower pressure. So the pressure on top of the wing is lower than underneath - and that pressure difference lifts the plane upward.

But that's only half the story.

Wings also push air downward. And according to Newton's Third Law, every action has an equal and opposite reaction. So if the wing pushes air down, the air pushes the wing - and the whole plane - up.

That's the real magic of flight:
Lift = Bernoulli's pressure difference + Newton's momentum exchange.

Add powerful jet engines that provide thrust, stabilizers that help with balance, and control surfaces (like flaps and rudders) that adjust angle and direction - and you have controlled, sustained flight.

You're not just flying.
You're riding a symphony of math, air pressure, and Newtonian precision - at 900 km/h.

As your tires hum along the asphalt and your mind drifts toward the day ahead, something catches your eye - a speed radar box, quietly watching.

Maybe you slow down instinctively, even if you're not speeding. But have you ever wondered how these silent, unblinking boxes actually detect your speed?

Speed cameras don't rely on magic - they rely on physics, and often, on photons.

There are two main types of radar-based speed measurement:

1. Doppler Radar (Radio Waves)

Most traditional speed radars use the Doppler effect, the same principle that makes a siren sound higher-pitched as it approaches you and lower as it moves away.

Here's how it works:

- The radar sends out radio waves toward your car.

- These waves bounce back off the moving vehicle.

- If your car is stationary, the frequency of the returned waves matches the sent waves.

- If you're moving, the frequency shifts - and the difference between sent and received wave frequencies tells the system how fast you're going.

This is the Doppler shift - the same principle astronomers use to measure the movement of stars and galaxies.

2. Laser Speed Guns (LIDAR)

Newer systems use LIDAR - Light Detection and Ranging. These send out short bursts of laser light (photons).

Here's how it works:

- The LIDAR unit emits rapid pulses of infrared light (photons).

- These photons reflect off your vehicle and return to the sensor.

- The system calculates distance over time for each pulse - and from that, determines your speed.

So yes - in LIDAR systems, photons measure your speed. They fly out at the speed of light, bounce off your car, and return. By timing this round trip precisely, the system knows how far you've traveled in a fraction of a second. Multiply that over several pulses - and it knows your velocity.

Why It's So Precise?

- These systems are extremely accurate - often measuring speeds within ±1 km/h.

- They work in daylight, darkness, and light rain.

- And because they use light or radio waves - they work instantly.

So the next time you pass a speed camera and it flashes - it's not a random trigger. You've just been scanned by a device using quantum particles or electromagnetic waves to catch a moment in time.

Arriving at Work: Chips, Codes, and Everyday Magic:

Once you arrive at work, you park your car and head to the building entrance.
Sometimes, you don't even need a key - just a chip.

These chips are the modern building blocks of our economy. Small but powerful. They're embedded with data that identifies you. When you hold your chip to the scanner, the system accesses a database to check whether you're an authorized employee.

If yes? Access granted.
If not? The door stays shut.
It feels automatic, but behind it is a mix of radio-frequency identification

(RFID), code, and logic gates - essentially tiny yes/no decisions happening in milliseconds.

You walk up the stairs - and in doing so, you're using kinetic energy again. In fact, if we could harvest that energy, just a few steps could power a lightbulb for a few seconds. Your body is an energy machine, even before you start working.

A single 75 kg person climbing one 20 cm stair burns ≈ 1.5 joules.
(energy is being measured in joules
Climbing 10 stairs = 15 joules.
A typical LED bulb uses about 10 watts, or 10 joules per second.
→ So 15 joules = enough to power a 10-watt bulb for 1.5 seconds.

Now you're in the office. Around you:
Monitors. CPUs. Keyboards. A mouse.
Every device runs on electricity - and underneath that, on code.

Your desktop PC is basically a box full of electrons, guided by instructions. These instructions are programs, and they're all written using code - languages like Python, C++, or JavaScript. But no matter the language, at the lowest level, it all breaks down to binary:
1s and 0s.

The entire digital world - texts, photos, music, videos, even this book - runs on a language of just two symbols: 0 and 1. Why?

Because computers are built from electronic switches - tiny transistors that can be either on or off.
That's it.
Just two states:

- 1 = on (electricity flows)

- 0 = off (no electricity)

This system is called binary code - the most efficient way for machines to process information.

But how does that turn into something like the letter A or a selfie or a voice message?

Well, each letter on your keyboard has a unique binary number assigned to it. For example:

- The letter A is 01000001

- The letter B is 01000010

- The letter C is 01000011

Each sequence of eight 0s and 1s is called a byte, and a computer translates those sequences into characters, colors, pixels, sounds - everything you see and hear on a screen.

Think of it like LEGO bricks: each individual piece is simple, but when arranged in the right pattern, they can build an entire castle.
In the same way, billions of 0s and 1s can represent a high-definition movie, a Zoom call, or this page.

It's one of the most powerful ideas in modern technology:
You don't need infinite symbols to express complexity - just two, combined in brilliant ways.

Imagine a giant book of formulas.
Each line of code is like a formula with a rule. For example:

If input = 2 + 2 → output = 4.
Unless... the programmer decides: 2 + 2 = 5. (Yes, it's possible - that's logic manipulation.)

Computers don't "know" truth.
They follow the instructions we give them - and those instructions define reality inside the machine.

No electricity = no flow of electrons.
No chips = no logic processing.
No code = no actions.

So that little blinking cursor on your screen? That's not just a symbol.
It's the tip of an iceberg made of silicon, energy, and human logic.

Online Meetings and IP Addresses:

If you have an online meeting, you'll typically click on a link - either from an email invitation or a calendar reminder. Behind that simple link is something powerful: an IP address.

Every device connected to the internet - including your laptop, phone, or the Zoom server - has an IP address. Think of it like a digital postal address. Just like the mail carrier needs an address to deliver a letter, the internet needs an IP address to send and receive data.

When you click a Zoom link, your device reaches out to Zoom's server using that address. Zoom then connects you to the right meeting, with the right people, in real time - often through dozens of connected servers.

But who assigns those addresses?

Your Internet Service Provider (ISP) gives your home or device a unique IP address when you go online. If you run a website, your hosting provider assigns it an IP address on their servers. These IPs are coordinated globally by organizations like ICANN and IANA to avoid duplication.

So every time you click, stream, or scroll - you're using invisible coordinates to talk to machines all around the world.

Why You Can't Just Make Up an IP Address?

(It's like trying to invent your own license plate)

Let's say you want your car to have the license plate "VIP-1234." Sounds cool, but... what if someone else already has it? What if millions of people picked their own plates?

That's why license plates - like IP addresses - are assigned by a central system.
The internet works the same way.

Every device needs a unique "address":

IP addresses are like your internet home address. When someone sends data to you - a message, a website, a video - it needs to know exactly where to go. If two people had the same IP? That data could go to the wrong person, or vanish.

Who decides these addresses?

The top-level system is run by ICANN and IANA, which coordinate address blocks globally. Then regional providers (like RIPE or ARIN) and your internet service provider (ISP) assign them to you.

You don't own the address - you borrow it, just like a license plate is tied to your car (not you forever).

But what about private networks?

You can choose your own IPs at home - like 192.168.1.1 - but only for your private Wi-Fi. These don't work on the public internet. They're like street names inside a gated community. Fine for internal use, but invisible to the outside world.

Final thought:

Without this organized system, the internet would be total chaos - imagine mailing a letter with no unique address. You'd never get your memes.

During your workday, you might not only jump into video calls - you might also need to make an old-school phone call. Maybe from your smartphone. But how does that even work? It's actually not too different from the internet. When you dial a number, your phone tries to connect to the nearest cell tower (or mast). That tower might be just outside your building - or hundreds of meters away. But how does your phone reach it? The answer: electromagnetic waves.

Your voice gets converted into electrical signals, which your phone transmits as radio waves. These waves travel invisibly through the air - just like Wi-Fi, Bluetooth, and even sunlight - until they hit the nearest tower. That tower picks up the signal, identifies the phone number you're trying to reach, and passes it through your mobile network provider. From there, it might travel through fiber-optic cables, data centers, or even undersea cables - until it gets routed to the country and tower nearest to the person you're calling. From there, the signal travels the last stretch - from their local tower to their phone. All this happens in milliseconds, at nearly the speed of light (about 300,000 km per second in a vacuum, slightly less through fiber). Your voice? It's riding on a wave of photons. Just like that, you're having a live conversation - with someone who might be thousands of kilometers away. And you didn't even have to yell.

Maybe it's 9:00 a.m. now - time for Znüni, as we call it in Switzerland. It's a small mid-morning break, and it's more than just a snack. It's a chance to connect - to talk with colleagues about work, life, or anything in between.

We humans love to interact. It's in our DNA. Our ancestors relied on social bonds to survive [3], and today, even in high-tech offices, that ancient instinct lives on.

During Znüni, most people have a coffee.
And that cup? It's a global story.

Coffee is made from roasted beans, often grown in countries like Honduras, Ethiopia, or Colombia. Why there? Because climate matters.

Coffee plants need warmth, humidity, and altitude - conditions found in the tropics, not northern Europe. [4]

The beans are usually harvested by hand, then roasted - a process that heats them to over 200°C. That's when the real transformation happens: chemical reactions (like the Maillard reaction) inside the beans create the rich aromas and flavors we know as coffee [5].

Today, more than 80% of the global population drinks coffee. [6] It's sometimes called "the fuel of the workforce."

Why?
Because coffee contains caffeine - a natural stimulant. It blocks adenosine (a molecule that makes you feel tired), and triggers a release of dopamine and adrenaline. [7] That's why coffee makes you feel more alert, focused, maybe even creative.

We crave stimulation. Without it, life can feel flat. But like anything powerful, it's about balance.
Moderate coffee = healthy. [8]
Too much = jittery.
Add smoking - even e-cigarettes - and the risk skyrockets.

Vape liquids can contain thousands of unknown chemicals - many of which have not been studied long-term. [9][10] So while coffee may be your friend in the morning, it's best enjoyed clean - no smoke required.

After you've worked your 8 hours - or more, depending where you live (in many parts of Asia, the workday is often longer) - it's finally time to clock out.

You do it for a paycheck - agreed upon when you signed your employment contract.
And so it continues, Monday to Friday, week after week.

At the end of each month, money lands in your account. And on the surface, it seems like a good system:
You work.

They pay.
Everyone's happy.

But here's the twist: even when people aren't happy, they often stay.
Why?

Some say it's responsibility.
Others: fear.
But many just say it's money.

We've all heard the phrase:

"The strongest drug in the world... is the salary."

And maybe it's true. Salaries offer safety. Stability. A reason not to risk.
They're like magnets.

Not in the physical sense - not like copper, magnetite, or neodymium.
But psychologically? Emotionally?
They pull people in.
They hold people in place.

And if we're not careful, we don't even notice we're being held.

You get one life.
And yet, many trade decades of it for security.
That's not necessarily wrong.
But it's worth asking:

"Is this what I want? Or am I just doing what I agreed to... a long
time ago?"

However each, up to there own.

But while the tech behind your workday might run like a machine, your
attention doesn't.

Most people spend their workdays reacting - jumping between emails,
Slack pings, calendar reminders, and sudden "Hey, can you just..."
interruptions.

That's urgency.
But urgency isn't importance.

It's the loudest voice in the room - not the one that moves your life forward.

If you spend all day swatting flies, you'll never build anything that flies. Real progress comes from focus - on the tasks that matter, even if they're quiet.

Want to build something meaningful? Prioritize what's important, not just what's immediate.

Ask yourself:

- Will this task matter in a week?

- Will it move the needle on my goals?

- Or am I just firefighting someone else's chaos?

Structure your day with intention.
Start with what's important, then handle the noise.

That's how you stop surviving your day - and start designing it. And very important if you are a boss: People do their best when they feel valued - not just paid. Incentives matter. They're the invisible forces that shape effort and behavior. When someone knows that their work is appreciated, that there's room to grow, and that success is possible, they give more. They become more. It's not just psychology — it's biology. The brain's dopamine system rewards progress and recognition. No incentives? No progress. But with the right incentives? Magic happens.

Chapter 3: In the City

It's Thursday, 4 p.m.

After work, I often like to go into the city. There's something magnetic about it - and that's not just personal. Humans are naturally drawn to other humans. Cities offer that: energy, variety, possibility.

In small towns or villages, everyone knows everyone. That creates comfort - but also limits. In cities, you don't just find more people - you find more types of people. That's why dating apps, meetups, and casual encounters tend to thrive in urban environments: scale equals choice.

As I arrive in the city, I circle to find parking. And I always wonder: "Should I keep searching or take this spot?" Surprisingly, there's a math-based strategy for that. It's part of optimal stopping theory, a concept from decision science that helps balance exploration and commitment. If all spots are free, take the best one. If about half are free, take the third one you see. If it looks almost full, take the first available. You're not just parking - you're doing applied mathematics.

In the city, people are drawn to many things: museums, music, food, shopping. But what succeeds most is atmosphere. The best restaurants, stores, and cafés don't just sell things - they create places people want to stay. It's not just "What should we hang on this wall?" but "What kind of place makes people linger?"

The same logic applies to business strategy. Don't ask, "Do I like this?" Ask, "Do others want to be here?" Even with great atmosphere, you still need a product that meets a need. Success is alignment: space, psychology, and market demand.

One of the most timeless urban experiences is the cinema. We don't just go for entertainment - we go for escape, emotion, and togetherness. And yet, it's all physics. A movie isn't motion - it's a sequence of still images, usually 24 per second, projected so quickly that your brain blends them into continuous movement. That illusion is called the phi phenomenon.

Light, or photons, beams through the projector to the screen. Block the beam, and the image disappears. No light means no story. And why do people return to sequels, remakes, or blockbusters? Because of social proof - a psychological effect where we assume something is valuable because others value it. It's how hits go viral. Cinemas don't just show stories - they create shared experiences.

Social proof doesn't stop at the movies. Go into a bookstore and most people head straight to the bestsellers. But if everyone's reading the same books, they're probably thinking the same thoughts. I remind myself: "If you only read what everyone else is reading, you'll end up thinking like everyone else."

Cities are full of hidden gems. Sometimes, that gem is a museum. I once saw an object that was over 20,000 years old - right there, in front of me. Perfectly preserved. No decay, no disintegration. Just... there. I remember thinking: "How can something that old still look like that?"

The answer is physics. Many ancient artifacts - bone tools, ivory carvings, stone weapons - are made from stable solid-state materials. Their atomic structures stay intact for thousands of years, as long as they're protected from heat, moisture, and pressure. Atoms don't decay on their own - they hold. That's how we can stand face-to-face with something from the Ice Age.

But museums aren't just science - they're emotion. In Munich, I once stood in front of an exhibit titled "The Garden of Eden." It felt like stepping into another world. Timeless. Dreamlike. In Vitoria-Gasteiz, Spain, I saw centuries-old paintings that asked more questions than they answered. What were they thinking? What did life look like then? Why this moment?

You don't just look at history. You feel it.

There's one more place in the city that deserves attention: the zoo. Why do we go to zoos? Because they let us stand face-to-face with the unfamiliar - lions, elephants, penguins, or gorillas - animals we'd rarely see in the wild. But they also raise serious questions. Should wild animals be kept in enclosures? Are zoos about learning... or just looking?

Both can be true. Zoos can inspire awe. They also ask us to take responsibility.

We forget: animals are made from the same stuff we are. Atoms become molecules, proteins, cells, bodies. They breathe, grow, feel. Some even grieve. They aren't just background scenery in a park - they're biological masterpieces, shaped by millions of years of evolution. Some scientists now argue that certain animals feel pain, anxiety, empathy - even sadness.

Do animals talk? Not in words. But yes - they communicate. Elephants mourn their dead - gently touching bones, revisiting gravesites, showing signs of distress. [1][2] Crows recognize and remember human faces, even warning others who to avoid. [3] Whales sing across oceans with complex sonic patterns, likely for mating or bonding. [4] Bees perform dances that relay food locations with shocking accuracy. [5] These aren't random behaviors - they're language, in forms we're only beginning to understand.

Do animals think about us? There's growing evidence they do. Crows pass down memories of human behavior. Primates react to fairness and generosity. Dogs and dolphins show empathy and self-recognition. They don't just observe - they assess.

Every species plays a role in nature. Pollinators. Predators. Pest controllers. Nutrient movers. But maybe animals also exist to remind us of something more: That life isn't just human. That intelligence isn't just verbal. That connection wears fur, feathers, or scales.

Next time you visit a zoo, don't just ask, "What kind of animal is that?"
Ask: "What do they know... that we don't?"
Are you looking at them - or are they looking back at you?

Chapter 4:

At the Amusement Park

It's Sunday, 8 a.m.

Amusement parks aren't just playgrounds for kids - they're science in motion.

Children love these places because they're wired for curiosity. They don't need to understand the mechanics of a ride to enjoy it - they just dive in. But behind the screams and excitement, there's a world of invisible forces at play: physics, biology, engineering, and chemistry.

Take Europa-Park in Rust, Germany. One highlight is the ice show - where a figure skater spins with a partner lifted overhead using just one arm. **How is that possible?**

It all comes down to angular momentum, the same principle that keeps satellites spinning in space. When the lifted partner keeps close to the center, it reduces what's called the moment of inertia, allowing the skater to spin faster while conserving angular momentum. That means: once the skater starts spinning, they don't need extra energy to keep going - the momentum stays constant unless acted on by an outside force.

And of course, roller coasters are the main attraction for thrill-seekers. Why do we love them? Because they trigger adrenaline, a hormone your body releases in exciting or risky situations. It boosts your heart rate, sharpens your senses, and gives you that electric rush.

On Europa-Park's famous Silver Star coaster, you can hit speeds over 130 km/h and experience up to 4 Gs of force.

But what does 4 G really mean?

G-force measures acceleration relative to gravity. 1 G is what you feel just standing on Earth. At 4 G, your body feels four times heavier. If you normally weigh 70 kg, your body feels like 280 kg pressing into your seat. Your muscles tighten, your vision narrows - it's intense, and it's all physics.

These rides begin with a lift hill, where mechanical work pulls the train upward - converting motion into potential energy. Once it crests the top, gravity converts that energy into kinetic energy as you drop, loop, and twist. You stay in your seat thanks to centripetal force - the inward force that keeps you moving in a circle instead of flying off the track.

And when the ride ends? That's where the real magic happens: electromagnetic braking.

Instead of using friction or pads, many coasters slow down using magnetic induction. As the ride passes over copper fins, magnets create a moving magnetic field. This field generates eddy currents in the copper, which in turn create an opposing magnetic force that slows the train - all without contact. It's silent, smooth, and incredibly efficient.

This tech is rooted in Faraday's Law of Induction, discovered in 1831 by Michael Faraday, and later explained by James Clerk Maxwell. Their work gave us the foundation for electric motors, generators - and yes, even your wireless phone charger.

How does a phone charger use the same principle? Simple: a coil inside the charger creates a magnetic field. That field induces an electric current in another coil inside your phone. No wires, no plugs - just induction.

In fact, some modern roller coasters use linear induction motors to launch trains at high speeds without any chains or cables. These motors work like maglev trains: magnets and copper coils pushing against each other to create powerful, controlled acceleration.

So yes - amusement parks are fun. But they're also full of physics.

And that physics doesn't stop at the park gate.

We use the same principles in airplanes, spacecraft, and even car crash safety systems. G-forces, angular momentum, magnetic braking - it's all around us.

We play with physics in amusement parks.

But we live by it every day.

And of course - what's a day at the amusement park without ice cream?

It's not just a treat - it's a little miracle of chemistry and physics.

Ice cream may look simple, but it's actually a complex mix of frozen water, milk fats, sugars, proteins, and - surprisingly - air. Yes, the smooth texture you love is partly due to millions of tiny air bubbles whipped into the mixture before freezing.

Without those bubbles, ice cream would be dense like an ice cube. With them? It becomes soft, fluffy, and scoopable.

And yes - it's made of atoms, just like everything else. But in this case, it's atoms forming molecules, which then come together into crystals, emulsions, and foams. It's dessert... designed by science.

No wonder ice cream is one of the most consumed snacks in amusement parks worldwide. It's cold, it's sweet, and it's a beautiful example of food science - right there in your hand.

Chapter 5: On the Trail

It's Sunday, 1 p.m. - and we've decided to go for a hike.

We drive to the mountains and park near a cable car. The air is fresh. The scenery is peaceful. But what makes hiking truly powerful isn't just the view - it's what it does to your body and mind.

Walking is one of the simplest, most effective forms of exercise. Just 5,000 steps a day can improve cardiovascular health, strengthen muscles, and support your mental well-being. But even more important is where you walk. Being in nature - away from cars, noise, and pollution - exposes you to clean air, natural light, and calm surroundings. That's a boost not just for your lungs, but for your nervous system too.

Don't forget a cap or sun cream. Why? Because sunlight includes ultraviolet (UV) radiation, and too much UV-B exposure damages your skin - leading to faster aging, or even skin cancer. Even inside a cable car, you're exposed to UV rays unless the windows are specially treated.

Sunlight might seem simple, but it's one of the universe's most incredible gifts.

It travels to Earth as photons - particles of light moving at 299,792,458 meters per second. These photons are generated in the Sun's core through nuclear fusion. But here's the amazing part: it takes those photons up to 100,000 years to escape the dense plasma of the Sun's interior. Once they're finally free, they race toward Earth in just over 8 minutes - and land on your skin, warming your face as you hike.

In a way, you're feeling the energy of an ancient journey.

And that light? It bends. Not by much - but by enough. Einstein showed us that gravity can bend light, and the Sun's mass curves space-time just enough for that to happen. This isn't science fiction - it's been observed in solar eclipses and confirmed by telescopes.

Now think about this: the Earth orbits the Sun, just as electrons orbit around atomic nuclei. It's not a perfect match, but the symmetry is poetic. Electrons are incredibly small - over 1,800 times lighter than protons - and yet they define how atoms behave. You can't see them directly, but powerful instruments like electron microscopes allow us to detect their paths.

And sunlight? Though it looks white or yellow to our eyes, it's actually a mix of many wavelengths - red, green, and blue light blended together. What we see as "color" is just our brain's way of interpreting different wave frequencies of electromagnetic radiation.

Back to the hike.

You step into the cable car. It moves steadily upward - suspended by a thin cable, but strong enough to carry tons of weight. And here again, physics is at work.

Cable cars use a combination of mechanical systems and electromagnetic force to move. Electric motors create rotating magnetic fields that drive wheels and pulleys - similar to the magnetic induction that slows down roller coasters, powers maglev trains, or even charges your smartphone wirelessly.

So while you're enjoying the mountain air, stretching your legs, and taking in the view - remember:
You're walking through a masterpiece of nature, powered by sunlight, governed by physics, and built by human engineering.

You're not just hiking.
You're traveling through science - one step at a time.

What Is a Photon - and Is It Made of Anything?

A photon is a particle of light - the smallest possible unit of electromagnetic energy.

But unlike protons or electrons, photons are not made of anything smaller. They're not built from protons, neutrons, or electrons. In fact:

- A photon has no mass

- A photon has no electric charge

- A photon is not made of atoms or subatomic particles

- A photon always travels at the speed of light

It's a fundamental particle - meaning it's one of the building blocks of nature that cannot be broken down further.

Photons carry the electromagnetic force - which includes light, radio waves, X-rays, UV rays, and even Wi-Fi signals. Without photons, we wouldn't see anything, plants couldn't photosynthesize, and the universe would be dark and silent.

So the next time you feel the warmth of sunlight - you're feeling a 13.5-billion-year-old photon journey, hitting your skin... with zero mass, but massive impact.

As we ride up the cable car, I glance down - trees stretch like a green carpet beneath us. To the right, cows are grazing lazily in a meadow. It's quiet, peaceful, and somehow full of questions.

How can cows eat grass - even with dirt on it?

Cows are biological marvels. They're ruminants, meaning they have a four-chambered stomach specially evolved to digest tough, fibrous plants like grass. Even if it's sprinkled with soil, no problem. Inside their stomachs, billions of microbes help break down cellulose - the main component of plant cell walls. What we'd struggle to digest, they turn into energy. Think of it as a built-in fermentation lab.

And what about the trees? How do they grow so tall? And why don't they grow even taller - like skyscrapers?

Tree height is governed by physics. To survive, a tree must transport water from its roots up to its highest leaves. This happens through thin vessels called xylem, using a mix of capillary action, cohesion between water molecules, and the pulling force of evaporation from the leaves (a process called transpiration). But this method has a physical limit.

Once a tree hits about 130 meters, gravity and resistance in the xylem make it nearly impossible to lift more water to the top. No water = no growth. That's why trees don't just grow forever. Even the tallest redwoods (around 115 meters) are pushing nature's limits.

But why are the trees exactly where they are?

It's not random. Trees grow where conditions are right: where there's enough sunlight, moisture, nutrients in the soil, and space to spread. Seeds are carried by wind, water, animals, and even gravity. A squirrel might bury a nut and forget it. A bird might eat a berry and drop the seed somewhere new. Some seeds are so light they float on the breeze. Others are sticky and hitch a ride on fur or feathers.

When a seed lands in the right spot - with enough light, soil, and protection - it germinates. Roots dig downward. A shoot reaches upward. It becomes a sapling... and eventually, maybe, a towering tree.

But here's the twist: trees aren't just individuals. Forests are communities.
They support each other through underground networks of fungi, known as mycorrhizal networks. These networks connect tree roots like an internet, allowing them to share nutrients, water, and even information. Older, more established trees - sometimes called "mother trees" - can help younger ones grow by sending them sugars and signaling danger (like insect attacks or drought stress).

This isn't fantasy - it's real science.
The groundbreaking research behind this was led by Dr. Suzanne Simard, a forest ecologist from the University of British Columbia. In one of her studies, she showed that trees could send carbon to other trees through these underground fungal connections - even to different species. [1]

So the next time you walk through a forest, remember:
Those trees aren't just growing.
They're talking, helping, warning, and cooperating. They're alive - and they're connected.

Even onions have a defense system. When you slice them open, they release a chemical called syn-Propanethial-S-oxide - a volatile compound that wafts upward and irritates your eyes. It's their way of "shouting" at your face to stop. It's not just random pain: it's biochemical warfare. Plants, though rooted in place, have evolved incredibly sophisticated protection strategies - from thorns and toxins to chemical messengers and partnerships with fungi. They're not passive. They're brilliant in their own way.

As we arrive at the station, we grab a drink - then set off on foot toward a mountain hut (an Alp or Hütte), about 1.5 hours away.

Soon, it begins to rain. Clouds hang low around the peaks. I'm mesmerized by them - they look like floating vapor, and in a way, they are.

Clouds are water droplets suspended in air - a gas state where particles are spread far apart. You can walk through a cloud and barely feel it, because the droplets are tiny, and the molecules are loosely packed. Rain is part of a giant cycle: water evaporates from lakes, oceans, and rivers; it condenses into clouds; when clouds get too heavy, they release moisture as rain.

With clouds forming, air pressure drops. And that drop - even if subtle - affects daily life. If you're cooking at high altitude (lower pressure), water boils at a lower temperature. That means your coffee or tea brews faster. Even the aroma might change.

Why? Lower pressure means fewer air molecules, including fewer electrons interacting with your surroundings. Water molecules move more freely and boil at a lower temperature. Science... in your cup.

As we walk through the rain, something surprising happened: I felt incredible.

Why does walking in light rain feel so good? Maybe it's the cooler air, or the rhythm of water droplets hitting your skin and jacket. Or maybe it's something deeper - a connection to nature that taps into our biology. Studies have shown that walking in nature, especially during or after rainfall, can lower cortisol (the stress hormone), boost endorphin levels, and increase what's called "parasympathetic activity" - the body's calming system. [2]

The rain refreshes everything. The scent of wet grass, damp soil, and pine trees fills the air - it's called petrichor, a term for that earthy smell after rain, caused by oils released from soil and bacteria. It's one of nature's most comforting aromas.

After about 90 minutes, we arrive at a small mountain hut - an Almhütte.

Inside, it's warm. Wooden benches. A stove in the corner. The sound of rain tapping softly on the roof.

I sit down and order a classic alpine snack: Käsebrot - a slice of dense bread with aged cheese - and a small beer.

It tastes perfect.

But even this moment? It's a science story.

That cheese? It started as milk from a cow like the ones we saw grazing earlier. Cows turn grass into milk using their four-chambered stomachs. Once collected, the milk is often pasteurized - gently heated to kill harmful bacteria. Then, enzymes and bacteria are added to ferment it. As the proteins coagulate and water (whey) separates out, the result is a soft curd. After aging for weeks or months, the cheese becomes firm, rich, and ready to enjoy.

Every bite contains proteins (like casein), fats, and minerals - but also microbial life, shaped by time, temperature, and bacteria. Fermentation turns milk into flavor.

And the beer?

It began as grain - barley or wheat - which is soaked, sprouted, and dried. During brewing, the grain is mixed with water and heated. Enzymes in the grain convert starches into sugars. Then yeast is added, which eats the sugar and releases alcohol and carbon dioxide.

That simple glass of beer is powered by biology and chemistry: enzymes, microbes, and fermentation - working together.

So yes: I was sitting in a small hut in the mountains, eating cheese and drinking beer. But what I was really experiencing was the result of ecosystems, fermentation science, agriculture, and human tradition... all on a wooden plate.

And it tasted even better in the rain.

Chapter 6: With Others

It's Sunday evening, 6 p.m.

You've got Monday off.

You step out - maybe to a bar, a cozy lounge, somewhere relaxed. You sit down, sip your drink, glance around. People are talking. Laughing. Meeting. Connecting.

Should you start a conversation?

That feeling - the impulse to connect - is one of the deepest human instincts.

Since the time of Neanderthals, we've depended on others to survive. Companionship wasn't just emotional - it was essential for safety, food, and belonging. We evolved as social beings. [1]

And today, we still crave fellowship - not just for romance or family, but even in passing interactions. A friendly exchange. A shared joke. A spark of understanding.

There are many reasons we talk:

- To exchange information

- To ask for help

- To persuade

- Or simply to connect for fun

But connection doesn't just happen.

Studies show that only about 18% of people mentally prepare for important conversations - like dates or interviews. [2] But visualizing these moments in advance builds confidence, and reduces anxiety.

Confidence is important - but connection is everything.

And that's especially true in romantic relationships.
Many people think the goal is to impress. But in reality, the most
powerful green light in any romantic relationship is feeling safe to be
yourself.
It's not about being perfect. It's about being comfortable, relaxed, and
accepted in someone's presence.

And eye contact? It's one of the fastest ways to build trust.

Looking into someone's eyes activates parts of the brain linked to
empathy and emotional understanding. It lowers defenses, fosters
connection, and signals authenticity.

In fact, studies show that sustained eye contact can synchronize heart
rates between two people - literally bringing hearts closer.

If you want to reach someone's mind - speak well.

But if you want to reach their heart - look them in the eye.

Because real connection goes beyond the first glance.

Good conversation helps build that.

That's the real test:
Can you be your full self - and still feel liked?
When the answer is yes, that's the beginning of something real.

And being good at it doesn't mean talking more - it means being present:

- Ask thoughtful follow-up questions

- Show genuine interest

- Use the other person's name - research shows we're neurologically
  tuned to respond positively to hearing it [3]

Most people stay on the surface - weather, work, weekend plans. But connection grows in depth. Ask real questions: "What excites you these days?" "What's something you've changed your mind about recently?"

Deep talk builds deep trust. It's the fast lane to emotional connection.

It also helps to understand how talking actually works.

What we casually call "speaking" is a chain of physical events:

- Your brain forms a thought

- Your lungs push air through your vocal cords

- Your lips and tongue shape that air into sound waves

- Those waves travel through space, hit someone's eardrum, become electrical signals... and are decoded into meaning

That's not just social behavior - it's quantum physics meets biology. [4]

And if you're in sales, business, or leadership - communication becomes even more vital.
Because people buy you before they buy your product.
Your enthusiasm, confidence, and ability to listen all shape trust.

Dale Carnegie knew this. He famously said:

"You can make more friends in two months by becoming interested in other people than in two years by trying to get other people interested in you." [5]

And science backs him up.
Our brains contain mirror neurons - specialized cells that fire both when we do something and when we see someone else do it. That's how we

"catch" emotions like enthusiasm, empathy, or confidence from others.
[6]

So remember this:

In any relationship - romantic, professional, or social - what matters most isn't saying the perfect thing.
It's being fully present.
It's creating a space where both people can relax, share, and feel safe.
It's about being yourself - and letting others do the same.

And if you want to connect quickly with someone? Make them laugh.

But how does humor work? Why do we laugh?

Because something surprises us. The brain expects one thing - and then it gets something else.

That mismatch - the twist, the unexpected - triggers joy.

That's the core of comedy. And here's the truth:
Everyone can be funny.
You don't need to be a stand-up comic or memorize jokes. Just say something slightly unexpected - or frame the obvious in a new, quirky way.

A playful comment. A sharp observation. A moment of self-deprecating honesty.

Humor isn't a gift - it's a choice to look at life from a funnier angle.
And when you do that, others can't help but smile.

Chapter 7: Inside the Body

Every moment you breathe, blink, digest, and think, your body performs a symphony of invisible miracles. While you sleep, it works. While you run, it adapts. Without asking your permission, it keeps you alive, processing information, creating energy, and healing itself. This quiet masterpiece of biology is not just maintenance; it's a 24/7 concert of systems designed for your survival.

The Heart: Relentless and Rhythmic:

Your heart never takes a day off. Beating around 100,000 times a day, it pumps blood through 60,000 miles of blood vessels, delivering oxygen and nutrients to every cell. This cardiac muscle is an automatic marvel, governed in part by the autonomic nervous system. It speeds up during a run, slows down during sleep, and adjusts instantly to your environment-without a conscious thought.

Surprising fact: Over an average lifetime, your heart will beat more than 2.5 billion times-without ever needing to be rebooted.

The Brain: Your Command Center:

Rewire your mind: Learning even a single new word each day reshapes your brain. This small act stimulates your neurons to form new connections, reinforcing the brain's plasticity and enhancing cognitive function over time.

Your brain is made of approximately 86 billion neurons. These are specialized cells-yes, cells, made up of atoms-that transmit electrical signals. Every thought, movement, emotion, and memory is built on the network of connections between neurons. When you learn something new, like a language or musical instrument, your brain actually grows new connections in a process called neuroplasticity. Even just attempting to learn can thicken your brain's gray matter. [1]

And don't underestimate the power of a good walk. Walking not only boosts cardiovascular health, it also stimulates brain activity, enhances mood, and improves memory. A study from Stanford University showed that walking increased creative output by 60%. [2] Your brain loves movement because it evolved to move through complex environments, not just to think in them.

Night Work and Your Brain:

Working night shifts can seriously disrupt your circadian rhythm - the internal clock that regulates sleep, hormones, body temperature, and brain chemistry. When this rhythm is off-balance, your risk of chronic fatigue, metabolic disorders, and even depression increases.

Long-term night work has been linked to higher rates of mood disorders, immune system suppression, and even some cancers. Your biology is designed for daylight activity and nighttime rest.

Fight that rhythm too long, and your mental and physical health may quietly suffer.

Did you know? Even when you're doing "nothing," your brain is highly active. This is thanks to the Default Mode Network (DMN), a system of interacting brain regions that becomes active when you're not focused on the outside world. It kicks in during rest, introspection, memory recall, and daydreaming-making it a breeding ground for creativity, self-reflection, and problem-solving.

Many people build mental castles - safe, rigid structures of belief that resist change. But truth doesn't live in comfort. Growth means tearing down walls and letting new perspectives in.

But why do people resist new ideas? One big reason: confirmation bias. It's the brain's habit of looking for information that agrees with what we already believe - and ignoring or downplaying anything that doesn't. This makes us feel safe... but stuck. If you only read, hear, and watch things that match your views, you won't grow - you'll just dig deeper into old patterns. To learn, you have to challenge your own thinking. Curiosity starts where certainty ends.

The Gut: Your Second Brain:

It may surprise you to know that your gut has its own nervous system-called the enteric nervous system-often referred to as the "second brain." It contains over 100 million nerve cells and communicates constantly with your central nervous system. This is why gut health and mental health are so intertwined. The microbiome, the vast collection of bacteria in your digestive system, also plays a role in mood regulation, immunity, and even decision-making. According to research published in Nature Reviews Neuroscience, gut bacteria can influence the production of neurotransmitters like serotonin. [3]

Analogy: Think of your gut as a bustling city of microbes-billions of microscopic residents working shifts, producing chemicals, and chatting constantly with headquarters (your brain).

Your Cells: The Unsung Heroes:

Every part of your body - skin, muscle, blood, brain - is made of cells. You are a walking symphony of about 37 trillion animal cells, each alive, busy, and self-sustaining.

Inside each cell is a tiny organelle called the mitochondria - the powerhouse of the cell.

Fun twist? Scientists believe mitochondria were once free-living bacteria, absorbed by early cells over a billion years ago - a theory called endosymbiosis, now widely supported in biology. [4]

It takes the glucose from your food and the oxygen you breathe, and transforms them into ATP (adenosine triphosphate) - the universal energy currency of your body. ATP powers everything: your heartbeat, your thoughts, your movement, even the blink of your eye.

And yes - all cells, including mitochondria, are made of atoms: carbon, hydrogen, oxygen, nitrogen, phosphorus. Molecules like DNA and proteins are just atoms arranged in meaningful patterns.

But here's something surprising:

The atoms in you - especially carbon - are the same ones found in diamonds.

Diamonds may seem exotic or rare, but they're simply carbon atoms arranged in a highly organized crystal lattice. That's it. What looks like a luxury gem is just a different pattern of something already inside you.

Your body is built with carbon - the same basic element. The difference? Arrangement. Pressure. Time.

And now, science is discovering something even wilder: nanodiamonds - tiny diamond particles - may help deliver drugs across the blood-brain barrier, offering hope for treating neurological conditions like Alzheimer's, glioblastoma, or Parkinson's. [5] The carbon that builds both your cells and diamonds might soon carry medicine into the mind.

So next time you see a diamond in a store window - or a molecule in your own cell - remember:

It's not the material that makes it special. It's the structure.

And what seems rare may just be familiar, rearranged.

But not all cells in nature are the same.

Plant Cells vs. Animal Cells: Two Versions of Life:

Plant cells have extra tools that animal cells don't. The most famous? Chloroplasts.

- Chloroplasts are plastids - specialized compartments inside plant cells.

- They contain chlorophyll, the green pigment that captures sunlight for photosynthesis.

- Chlorophyll absorbs red and blue light but reflects green wavelengths - and that's what we see.

Color isn't a property of objects themselves - it's a perception. When light hits an object, some wavelengths are absorbed while others bounce off. Those reflected wavelengths enter your eye, strike specialized cells in your retina called photoreceptors, and trigger electrical signals to your brain. That's where color happens - not in the object, but in you.

Human eyes have three types of color-sensitive cones: short (which detect blue), medium (green), and long (red) wavelengths. Your brain blends input from these cones to construct the experience we call color. You don't see light itself - you experience your brain's interpretation of electromagnetic frequencies. That's why a tree looks green: it reflects green wavelengths and absorbs the others. But green isn't in the tree. It's the name your mind gives to that specific interaction of light and biology.

It's the same with ink. When you use a red pen, you're not writing "redness" onto the page. The ink contains dye molecules - often azo compounds or quinacridones - that absorb certain wavelengths and reflect red ones. The difference between red and blue ink comes down to molecular structure: different molecules reflect different parts of the spectrum. Your brain handles the rest.

Color, then, is not something painted onto the world. It's a conversation between physics, chemistry, and perception. It's your brain's way of turning invisible energy into experience - into emotion, memory, and meaning.

And here's a bonus insight: some animals, like mantis shrimp, have up to 12 types of color receptors compared to our three. Their brains may construct a reality filled with hues we'll never see - a rainbow with layers we can't even imagine.

Chloroplasts in plants don't just power photosynthesis. They shape the color of the natural world. They absorb red and blue light, and reflect green. So when you look at a forest, you're seeing frequencies the trees rejected - filtered light, decoded by your eyes, and turned into beauty by your brain.

Different life forms. Same sunlight. Different hardware. Same photons. And in that shared light, we find a common language - written not in words, but in wavelengths.

You and trees share something amazing: you're both made of cells powered by inner energy engines - mitochondria in your body, chloroplasts in leaves. Both types of cells are made from atoms forged in stars. You're different versions of the same cosmic recipe.

The Hidden Dangers in Your Water:

What enters your body doesn't start with food - it often starts with water. In Flint, Michigan, toxic lead levels weren't just a crisis - they were a warning. Infrastructure failure affected thousands of brains, especially children's developing minds.
And it's not just lead. In many rural regions, nitrates seep into well water from fertilizers. High nitrate levels have been linked to thyroid disease, cancer, and birth defects.
Then there's PFAS - "forever chemicals" used in non-stick cookware, waterproof fabrics, and fast-food wrappers. They linger in the bloodstream for decades and are linked to liver damage, infertility, and immune suppression.

The good news? Advanced filtration systems - such as those using activated carbon, reverse osmosis, or ion exchange - can significantly reduce PFAS levels in drinking water. While not every household filter does the job, certified filters tested to NSF/ANSI standards can make a big difference.

You might never see these threats. But your cells remember them. Clean water isn't a luxury - it's biology's foundation.

Want to Feel Better? Start with Food:
A 2013 study found that eating just two kiwis per day for two weeks significantly increased energy and reduced fatigue. [6]
Why? Kiwi is loaded with vitamin C and antioxidants that support your brain and gut.
And it's not alone.

- A few squares of dark chocolate can boost serotonin and reduce stress.

- Fermented foods like kefir, yogurt, or kimchi nourish your gut - your second brain.
  Nature isn't just fuel - it's medicine.

Another brain-booster: Omega-3 fatty acids - especially DHA.

These essential fats play a critical role in brain development, memory, and cognitive performance. In fact, a 2013 meta-analysis published in PLOS ONE found that omega-3 supplementation was associated with improved executive function and learning, particularly in children and older adults with low baseline intake. [7]

And it goes beyond the brain. Two simple nutrients can make a big difference in how you feel - and how you age: Vitamin D and Omega-3 fatty acids. Vitamin D - produced when sunlight hits your skin - supports your immune system, bones, and mood. Many people, especially in northern climates, don't get enough. Omega-3s (like DHA) are essential for heart health and reducing inflammation. And now we know: these nutrients don't just support health — they can actually slow biological aging. In randomized studies, vitamin D (2,000 IU — about one capsule, since food and sunlight alone often aren't enough), combined with omega-3 and exercise, slowed the body's aging clock by almost three years. [8] Simple tools. Real science.

Everything Connects:

The magic of your body lies in its interconnectedness. The brain talks to the gut. The gut influences mood. The heart responds to the brain. The cells fuel them all. And you? You're the conductor of this orchestra, whether you know it or not.

Want to support this miraculous system?

- Try learning a new language or hobby.

- Take a daily walk.

- Eat real, whole foods that support your gut.

- Sleep well to give your brain and cells time to recover.

Don't just chase goals - chase moments that move you. Go to a concert and let the bass shake your chest. Dance badly. Laugh until your ribs hurt. These experiences do more than entertain - they light up your brain's reward system, reduce stress hormones, and even boost your immune response. Emotions are physical, not just mental. And these moments stick far longer in your memory than anything you'll ever order online.

You're not just living in your body. You're alive because of it. And every system, from neuron to heartbeat to gut flora, is working quietly and tirelessly to keep it that way.

You are a living miracle-not because of what you know, but because of the living network inside you that never stops knowing how to keep you alive.

Isn't it extraordinary? I wonder - who could have created such an incredible system?

How is it that we function so precisely, so elegantly, every single day?

Chapter 8: Inside the Mind

Your mind works around the clock. It doesn't pause when you sleep-it simply shifts gears. At night, the subconscious mind takes the wheel, processing your memories, emotions, and unresolved thoughts through dreams and neural consolidation. During the day, however, your mind operates in two distinct modes: autopilot and active control.

Two Modes of the Mind:

Think about your commute to work. If you take the same route every day, there's a good chance you don't even remember parts of the drive. That's because you're in System 1-the fast, intuitive, automatic mind. [1] This is your subconscious, and it's incredibly efficient. It manages habits, routines, and responses without effort.

But when you make a decision, write a message, or solve a problem, you're engaging System 2-the conscious, slow, deliberate mode. It requires effort and energy. Nobel laureate Daniel Kahneman described this dual system in his groundbreaking book Thinking, Fast and Slow. [1]

Interestingly, up to 95% of our daily actions and decisions are made by the subconscious mind. [2] That means most of your life is lived on autopilot.

Where Is the Mind?

Scientifically, the mind doesn't reside in a single place. It's considered an emergent property of the brain-a dynamic process created by the firing of billions of neurons. But it's not just the brain. The gut and heart also influence the mind significantly.

- Your gut contains over 100 million neurons and produces up to 95% of your body's serotonin. [3]

- Your heart has its own complex neural network (the "heart-brain") and communicates with the brain via the vagus nerve. It can even predict and influence decision-making, especially under uncertainty. [4]

When we say "listen to your heart," there's science behind it. A study from the University of Cambridge found that people made more accurate decisions in ambiguous situations when they were better at detecting their own heartbeat-called interoceptive awareness. [4]

We Rarely Think Deeply.

Why Is It So Hard to Think?

Thinking-really thinking-is metabolically expensive. The brain uses up about 20% of your body's energy while only accounting for about 2% of your body weight. [5] System 2, the slow, effortful thinking process, is particularly draining. Your brain is wired to conserve energy, which is why it defaults to easier, quicker pathways-habits, assumptions, routines.

It's also emotionally difficult. Thinking forces us to confront uncertainty, make decisions, reflect on failures, and question beliefs. This creates discomfort. Our brains don't just seek truth-they seek comfort and safety.

Combine this with an attention-fragmented environment, and it becomes clear why deep thinking is rare. But it's also incredibly valuable. Real breakthroughs, meaningful change, and clarity come only when we engage that deeper part of the mind.

Shockingly, research suggests we truly think-deeply reflect or reevaluate our life choices-only two or three times a year. [6] Most of the time, we're reacting, coping, drifting.

And our discomfort with stillness is profound. In one study, 75% of people preferred giving themselves a mild electric shock rather than spending 15 minutes alone with their thoughts. [7] Another study found that the average person checks their phone over 150 times per day, constantly escaping silence. [8]

Our modern environment overwhelms the brain with input. A 2020 study estimated that we consume about 74 gigabytes of data per day-the equivalent of watching 16 movies daily. [9] But rarely do we pause to ask if all that input leads to better thinking.

The Curse of Procrastination:

Procrastination is one of the mind's greatest traps. Imagine a world where it didn't exist-how much progress could we have made? Studies show procrastination affects up to 20–25% of adults chronically and leads to lower income, reduced well-being, and even poorer health outcomes. [10]

The cure? It's simpler than we want it to be:

Take a pen. Start now.

That first micro-action dismantles the wall of avoidance. Momentum builds clarity. Neuroscience shows that starting a task releases dopamine, the brain's motivation chemical, which helps sustain focus and flow. [11]

The Tortoise Mind:

British psychologist Guy Claxton coined the term "tortoise mind" to describe the kind of slow, non-linear thinking that leads to creativity and wisdom-not speed. While we rush to "figure it out," often our best ideas emerge when we walk, doodle, or let go. [12]

Einstein famously said his breakthroughs came during walks or violin breaks-not in front of chalkboards. Studies confirm that the default mode network (DMN)-the brain system active during daydreaming-is deeply involved in creative insight and self-reflection. [13]

Intelligence Is Not Enough:

William Sidis, a man believed to have had an IQ over 250 - far beyond Einstein - is often cited as the smartest human to ever live. But brilliance alone doesn't guarantee success. Sidis lived reclusively, publishing under pseudonyms and avoiding fame. Intelligence is potential. What matters is how you use it.

Some people are born with extraordinary mental firepower - but even that doesn't guarantee a meaningful life.

Of course, how we think is only part of the equation. How we learn is just as crucial.

Speed Reading: A Mental Superpower:

Reading slowly isn't always better. In fact, one of the easiest ways to level up your learning is to train your eyes to jump. Speed reading isn't a trick - it's a shift. You scan lines in chunks, not words, letting your brain do the meaning-making. With just a little practice, you'll double your reading speed - and comprehension often increases, too. Speed readers don't just read more - they think faster, because they learn faster.

How Memory Works - and Why We Forget:

Your brain doesn't just store information like a hard drive. It constantly updates, deletes, and reshapes memories based on relevance and repetition.

In fact, according to the Ebbinghaus Forgetting Curve, you may forget up to 80% of what you learn within one month - unless you revisit or apply it.
This is your brain being efficient: it clears out unused data to make room for what matters.

Want to remember more?

- Revisit what you've learned within 24 hours.

- Apply the idea in real life.

- Teach it to someone else.

Learning isn't just about exposure - it's about reinforcement.
Repetition doesn't just help memory - it rewires your brain.

Think in Pictures - It's How You Learn Best:

Your brain doesn't absorb knowledge in plain text. It learns in images, scenes, and emotions. That's why the best way to remember something is to visualize it. Turn concepts into mental pictures - stories, shapes, or symbols - and you'll never forget them.

The Future You:

We rarely stop to ask: What does my ideal day look like? Instead, we drift through routines, settle into relationships out of habit, and miss the opportunity to live intentionally.

Most people spend more time planning a vacation than designing their life. But your future self is shaped by what you decide today.

You can think your way to a better life. Ask better questions.
Make space for silence.
Write down your future.
And walk toward it.

You're not just here to consume the world - you're here to shape it.

And with each moment of awareness, each page turned, each step taken-you build a better one.

Chapter 9: Under Influence

We are not born into a vacuum. From our earliest moments, we are shaped-quietly, powerfully-by others. Parents may set the stage, but neighbors, peers, media, culture, and language complete the script. Our identity is not built in isolation; it is sculpted by interaction.

Dopamine: The Invisible Hand:

This dopamine-driven cycle is central to how modern digital culture influences us. Social media platforms like Instagram and Facebook are built on variable reward systems-similar to slot machines. Every like, comment, or notification triggers a small dopamine hit, keeping us coming back for more. In fact, engineers at major platforms have acknowledged using reward loops and behavioral psychology to maximize engagement.

Dating apps operate on similar mechanics. They blend swiping with intermittent positive feedback (matches, messages), a technique borrowed from gambling psychology. You keep playing because maybe the next swipe will change your life-a classic dopamine trick.

Our culture is increasingly shaped by these invisible dopamine cycles. We're not just choosing what we like-we're being neurologically conditioned to seek it.

One of the brain's most influential forces in shaping behavior is dopamine. It's often called the "pleasure molecule," but that's misleading. Dopamine is less about reward and more about anticipation-the chase rather than the catch.

We don't feel our happiest when we achieve something-we feel our happiest before we achieve it. That pre-joy, that delicious sense of "almost," is what motivates us to move, build, chase, and dream.

Studies show that the brain releases more dopamine in anticipation of a reward than upon receiving it. [1] This explains why goals, dreams, and even crushes feel so powerful: our brain is lighting up before anything real has happened.

The Power of Social Proximity:

We are deeply shaped by those around us-not just emotionally, but behaviorally. Social proximity plays a massive role in how habits form. For example, we often start drinking alcohol because our friends do. We pick up smoking not in isolation, but in groups.

These are examples of social modeling-the tendency to adopt behaviors we observe in others, especially those we identify with. Humans are herd creatures. Belonging often feels more important than logic, and we'll do irrational things just to fit in.

Parents matter, but they're not the strongest force in long-term shaping. In fact, research shows that peers, neighbors, and close friends influence our behavior far more than family once we reach adolescence. [2]

- If your friends exercise, you're more likely to.

- If your neighbor quits smoking, your odds of quitting increase.

- If your social circle reads more, eats healthier, or takes risks-you will too.

Behavior is contagious. Our identities are social reflections as much as personal constructions.

Ever noticed how you clap when others do - even if you're not sure why?
One person starts, and suddenly the whole room joins in. It's not logic - it's wiring. We're tribal creatures. Our brains evolved to mirror others for survival.

We copy tone, posture, even decisions - often without realizing. Just one person looking up at the sky can make a whole crowd stop and stare.

Influence isn't just big. It's invisible.

It's not just friends who shape us - what we consume shapes us too.

Most people consume too much news. Not information - news. Endless updates on accidents, scandals, random events. But ask yourself: "Will knowing this change anything in my life?" For most stories, the answer is no. In fact, constant news can drain your attention and increase stress. Instead, choose intentional information - learn about your craft, your health, the economy, or topics that help you grow. Focus beats noise. You can't build your life on headlines.

Culture Teaches Us How to Be:

Are you kind because of who you are? Or because of how you were taught to be?

Chances are, your sense of right and wrong, politeness, and compassion were modeled for you before you could talk. Mirror neurons in the brain help us absorb social behavior. We smile when others smile. We feel embarrassment when others are shamed.

From classroom rules to cultural customs, we internalize values early-and they become us.

Researchers have found that when we observe someone smiling or showing fear, our own brain activates as if we're experiencing it ourselves-a function of mirror neurons. [3] This is why empathy is not just emotional-it's biological.

Cultures that emphasize shared stories, rituals, and values tend to persist longer-and more cohesively-than those that don't. Our shared narratives are the glue of civilization.

But if we're so wired for connection - why do we often make irrational choices?

Our minds are full of invisible mental traps...

Mental Traps: How the World Nudges You Without You Noticing:

Ever wonder why prices end in .99? It's not an accident - it's psychological. We read from left to right, so $4.99 feels like "four-something," not five.

Or take the sunk cost fallacy - we stick with bad investments, relationships, or projects just because we've "already spent so much." But time and energy already spent are gone. Only future return matters. Smart decisions require letting go.

Then there's anchoring - that first price you see shapes what feels "reasonable." And framing - we react differently to "90% fat-free" than "10% fat," even though they're the same.

We're wired to fear loss more than gain. To believe what's familiar, not what's true. And to follow crowds even when they're wrong.

The modern world is full of nudges. The trick? Notice them. Name them. And then choose for yourself.

Sometimes, we don't even realize we're saying "yes." In a now-famous psychology experiment, researchers asked people if they could cut in line at a copy machine. When they asked plainly, about 60% agreed. But when they added a meaningless reason - "because I need to make some copies" - that number jumped to over 90%. [4] Our brains heard the word "because" and defaulted to agreement, even though the reason added no value. We weren't deciding. We were reacting.

And it goes deeper. Neuroscientist Benjamin Libet found that our brains show electrical activity preparing for a decision up to half a second before we're consciously aware of having made one. [5] In other words: the decision is already in motion before "you" feel like you chose.

That's not a flaw - it's how your brain handles complexity. But it means some of what feels like free will is actually fast autopilot. And knowing that gives you power. Power to pause. Power to question. Power to make sure your "yes" is really yours.

Communication: The Great Shaper:

There are over 7,000 languages spoken today, but more than half the world's population speaks just 23 of them. [6] This reflects how cultural dominance-not just diversity-shapes the linguistic landscape.

Language is one of the most powerful tools of cultural influence-and one of the most underrated. The languages we speak didn't emerge overnight. They evolved over centuries through oral storytelling, migration, conquest, trade, and collaboration. Some languages faded away. Others merged. The ones that lasted are those that adapted-those that were spoken often, passed down, and woven into rituals and systems of power.

Interestingly, language tends to preserve what a culture values most. For example, some Arctic communities have dozens of words for snow, while others lack a word for privacy. This shows how language doesn't just reflect thought-it guides it. The words available to you shape what you can think, say, and feel.

Language also sticks through social imitation. We mimic the speech of those around us-parents, teachers, influencers. That's why accents, slang, and even opinions cluster in communities. We speak how we hear others speak, and in doing so, we pass on ideas and identities.

The way we speak and are spoken to also programs our minds. Words don't just describe our reality-they define it.

Language determines what we notice, how we remember, and how we solve problems. This is known as the linguistic relativity hypothesis-or more simply, the idea that language shapes thought. [7]

Just being exposed to certain ideas repeatedly-through news, social media, or stories-changes our beliefs over time. This is called the availability heuristic: we believe what's familiar, not necessarily what's true. [8]

Influence Is a Loop:

Here's the beautiful (and daunting) truth: we are shaped, and we shape.

Your decisions, your kindness, your courage-they influence others. Sometimes invisibly. Sometimes permanently.

You are both a mirror and a spark.

So choose your inputs wisely. Shape your circle carefully. And remember: the culture you're part of is also one you're helping to create.

You don't just live in culture. You carry it. You pass it. You shape the world with every word, gesture, and choice you make.

Chapter 10: The Bigger Picture

From local actions to global impact: systems, scale, and responsibility:

Changing the world sounds grandiose. But the truth is, world-changing doesn't begin on podiums or in parliaments-it starts in kitchens, classrooms, sidewalks, and screens. It begins with intention, scales with systems, and spreads through people.

The Butterfly Effect: Why Small Actions Matter:

A single idea, act of kindness, or post can ripple farther than you imagine. Scientists call this sensitive dependence on initial conditions-but most people know it as the butterfly effect. One small flap can eventually shift a storm.

Planting a tree in your neighborhood contributes to carbon sequestration. Choosing sustainable products influences supply chains. Teaching one child empathy creates generational ripple effects. Small is not small when multiplied. And not just through ripples - through growth.

One of the simplest and most powerful ideas in life is the compound effect - the "Zinseszinseffekt" in German. It's how small actions, repeated consistently, can create huge results over time. Just like money grows through compound interest, habits and learning grow through repeated effort. A few pages a day becomes a library. A few steps a day becomes strength. A few kind words a day becomes deep trust. Small things matter - because they grow. And when enough small changes connect? They reshape systems.

Think Systems, Not Symptoms:

Global problems - climate change, inequality, misinformation - aren't isolated. They're systemic. Which means solutions must address root structures, not just surface outcomes.

- Don't just donate to hunger relief; ask why food deserts exist.

- Don't just fight symptoms of inequality; question how laws, education, and access shape opportunity.

- Don't just recycle; vote for infrastructure that supports zero-waste systems.

Systems thinking invites us to zoom out, ask better questions, and look for leverage points-places where a small push creates big change.

Local Action, Global Impact:

Your most immediate power lies where you are. Research shows that social tipping points often begin in tight-knit communities. When just 25% of a group consistently upholds a belief or behavior, it can cause the majority to shift. [1]

This is how movements start. It's why community organizers matter. It's how cultural revolutions happen: someone acts differently-consistently-and others follow.

The Power of Example:

You are always leading someone - even if you don't know it. Whether you're a parent, a coworker, or a stranger on the street, your example matters.

Studies show that witnessing someone else engage in a pro-social behavior (like helping, volunteering, or even voting) dramatically increases the likelihood that we'll do the same. [2]

Your integrity is contagious. So is your courage. So is your silence.

Scale What Works:

Changing the world doesn't mean reinventing it. Often, the best progress comes from scaling solutions that already work:
A literacy program in one village, replicated in ten.
A renewable energy startup going global.
A local law becoming federal policy.

Look for what's already effective - and ask how to scale it without diluting its soul.

But well-intended actions don't always lead to the outcomes we hope for.

Things are often more complex than they seem.

Avoiding meat doesn't automatically reduce harm - especially if demand shifts to other forms of industrial farming with their own environmental costs.
Cutting back on tree use doesn't always protect forests - it can also remove financial incentives to plant and manage them sustainably.
What looks like progress in one corner can quietly cause damage in another.

Complexity matters. Systems interact. Change is rarely linear.
To create lasting impact, we have to think beyond quick fixes - and understand how parts affect the whole.

The Responsibility of Awareness:

The more you understand how influence works, the more power you hold. And with power comes responsibility. Not in the comic-book sense-but in the human sense.

Once you see how systems shape lives, you can't ignore the gears.
Once you know you can influence others, you can't pretend your actions are neutral.

The world doesn't just change from the top down - it transforms from the inside out.

Quantum Cats, Electric Realities, and the Code of Trust:

The closer you look at reality, the stranger it gets. From invisible particles that exist in two places at once to digital coins protected by math rather than banks, we are living in a world shaped by physics - and now, by code.

Welcome to the weird and wonderful intersection of quantum mechanics, technology, and trust.

Schrödinger's Cat - The Weirdest Thought Experiment:

Imagine ordering a package online. The moment it leaves the warehouse, you don't know if it's broken or intact. Until you open the box, it exists in both states - damaged and fine - in your mind.

That's what Erwin Schrödinger proposed with his cat in a box - a creature that is, in a quantum sense, both dead and alive until someone checks.

It's not about cruelty - it's about how weird reality gets when you zoom in close enough. Particles exist in superpositions - multiple states at once. Only when we observe them does a specific outcome become real.

Key lesson: Uncertainty isn't a flaw - it's how nature works.

In 2020, physicists created a real-life "quantum cat" using superconducting circuits. It existed in two different energy states at once-proving Schrödinger's thought experiment is now more than theory. The cat is still metaphorical, but the weirdness is very real.

Quantum Electrodynamics (QED) - Light, Matter, and Possibilities:

What happens when light hits matter? QED - Quantum Electrodynamics - is the most accurate theory ever developed.

When you touch your phone and it lights up, photons (light particles) interact with electrons in the screen. That's QED at work.

Light isn't just a wave - it's also a particle. Electrons react to those photons. That's how touchscreens, solar panels, and even your eyes function.

Mind-blower: Richard Feynman said QED can predict electron behavior so precisely, it's like measuring the distance from New York to LA with a margin of error smaller than a human hair.

From Quantum to Crypto - What Does This Have to Do with Bitcoin?

Cryptocurrencies like Bitcoin are decentralized digital currencies that use blockchain technology to validate and record transactions. Instead of relying on a central bank, the system runs on a distributed ledger maintained by thousands of computers worldwide.

Every transaction is verified using cryptographic algorithms. Here's how:

1. Your wallet creates a digital signature – It uses your private key to sign the transaction, proving it's authorized by you without exposing your key.

2. The transaction is broadcast to the network – Thousands of nodes (computers) receive it.

3. Miners (or validators) verify it – They confirm it fits the blockchain rules and isn't fraudulent. In Bitcoin's case, this means solving a complex math puzzle (proof-of-work).

4. Consensus is reached – If enough nodes agree, the transaction is added to the next block.

5. Finality and immutability – Once added, changing the block would require redoing the cryptography for all future blocks across the entire network-virtually impossible.

Anyone can create their own wallet by downloading an app or using a hardware device. This wallet contains your private/public key pair. Once created, you can send and receive crypto by connecting to the blockchain network via internet-connected software. Your wallet speaks to nodes, broadcasts transactions, and listens for confirmations - no bank required. Once verified, it's added to a chain of prior transactions - a blockchain. This ledger is publicly visible but tamper-proof, because changing one block would require changing all blocks on all computers at once.

New coins are created through a process called mining, where computers solve extremely difficult mathematical problems-a process grounded in computational probability.

Crypto works because it replaces human trust with mathematical proof.

In the quantum world, we collapse uncertainty by observing.
In crypto, we collapse distrust by verifying.
One collapses reality. The other collapses doubt.

Now back to our broader analogy:

If the quantum world is about uncertainty, crypto is about trust in uncertainty.

In quantum mechanics, we don't predict individual outcomes - we trust probabilities. In blockchain, we don't trust a single person - we trust math, encryption, and consensus.

Both rely on:

- Probability

- Information theory

- Observation and verification

Future quantum computers may break today's cryptographic systems. Here's how:

Traditional cryptography, like RSA or ECC (Elliptic Curve Cryptography), depends on mathematical problems that are practically impossible for classical computers to solve - such as factoring huge numbers or solving discrete logarithms. But quantum computers, using Shor's algorithm, could solve these problems exponentially faster.

What would take a classical computer millions of years could take a quantum computer mere hours or minutes.

That's why researchers are now developing post-quantum cryptography - encryption methods designed to resist attacks even from large-scale quantum machines. That's why researchers are building post-quantum cryptography right now.

Financial Systems - Trust, Value, and Illusion:

Let's zoom out even further. What does quantum uncertainty have to do with the global financial system? More than you'd think.

Money, at its core, is a story we all agree to believe. A $20 bill is just paper - until we all trust it has value. Modern banking is built on confidence and code, not just cash.

Here's how it works:

- Central banks issue money based on economic signals, not gold.

- Commercial banks loan out more than they physically hold-a system called fractional reserve banking.

- Markets move based on expectations, not certainties. (Sound familiar?)

Much like quantum physics, the financial system thrives on probability and behavior. The system works because we trust it to work.

Over $100 trillion circulates globally in various financial instruments-yet less than 8% of that exists in physical cash. The rest? Digital promises, ledgers, and belief.

As crypto, decentralized finance, and central bank digital currencies rise, the financial system is shifting from paper to protocol.

Quantum mechanics teaches us that uncertainty is baked into nature. Finance teaches us that trust can be coded.

The Physics of Change - Why Your Actions Matter:

In both physics and social systems, small inputs can have nonlinear effects. This isn't just metaphor-it's science.

In chaos theory, a tiny change in initial conditions can lead to radically different outcomes. This is mirrored in social tipping points and individual behavior. Just as a quantum measurement can alter a particle's path, your conscious choices influence complex networks of people, systems, and futures.

Amazing parallel: A single electron, influenced by observation, changes the outcome. A single person, acting with purpose, can alter cultural momentum.

We are all quantum nodes in the social field-connected, uncertain, and impactful.

Every act matters. Every vote, every word, every kindness collapses possibility into reality.

Quantum Fields, Semiconductors & Solar Power - The Fabric of Modern Life:

Before anything else, there are fields. In modern physics, Quantum Field Theory (QFT) tells us that particles aren't tiny balls-they're excitations in invisible fields that fill the universe. Every electron is a ripple in the electron field. Every photon? A wiggle in the electromagnetic field.

Everything you see, touch, and use arises from these quantum ripples.

Semiconductors: From Sand to Superpowers:

You might wonder: if quantum fields are dynamic and uncertain, why don't solid objects constantly shimmer and move? Why does your phone stay still? The answer lies in the emergent stability of quantum systems. At macroscopic scales, quantum chaos averages out. The atoms in a table don't jitter into chaos because the field interactions settle into low-energy, stable configurations-what we call solid matter.

This is especially true in crystalline solids like silicon, where atoms are arranged in a regular lattice. These structured fields allow us to engineer precision materials-like semiconductors.

Semiconductors are the foundation of the digital world. Found in smartphones, computers, cars, and satellites, they are made from carefully engineered crystals of silicon, refined from sand.

Semiconductors are the foundation of the digital world. Found in smartphones, computers, cars, and satellites, they are made from carefully engineered crystals of silicon, refined from sand.

What makes semiconductors special is their ability to switch states-from conducting electricity to blocking it. Using tiny transistors (often billions on a single chip), they form the logic gates that power all computing.

These chips are crafted using extreme ultraviolet lithography (EUV)-a technique that uses focused beams of light only 13.5 nanometers wide. The machinery that etches these patterns operates at a precision rivaling atomic spacing and costs billions of dollars per unit. The energy used to drive this process involves ultra-hot plasma that reaches over 220,000°C (400,000°F).

It's arguably the most advanced manufacturing process humans have ever created.

The latest chips contain features just 3 nanometers wide-20,000 times thinner than a human hair.

Solar Cells: Harvesting Quantum Light:

Solar panels are quantum machines. When sunlight hits a photovoltaic cell, photons strike electrons, knocking them loose from atoms and generating electricity.

This is called the photoelectric effect, which won Einstein the Nobel Prize. It's the very proof that light behaves as a particle.

From lighting homes to powering Mars rovers, solar energy is applied quantum physics-and one of the cleanest tools to fight climate change.

Mind-blower: Every hour, the sun beams more energy onto Earth than humanity uses in a year. Quantum physics gave us the tools to finally start capturing it.

How a Quantum Computer Works - Not Just Faster, But Different:

Quantum computers don't just do what classical computers do, but faster - they do things classical machines can't do at all.

Here's how:

- Instead of bits (which are 0 or 1), quantum computers use qubits. These can be 0, 1, or a superposition of both.

- Qubits can also be entangled, meaning changing one instantly affects the other, even if they're far apart.

- Quantum gates manipulate these qubits in a way that allows the computer to process many possibilities simultaneously.

In a classical computer, you try one password at a time. In a quantum computer, you try all of them at once (in a sense)-and then collapse the result down to the correct one through quantum interference.

Quantum computers are built with delicate systems like superconducting circuits, trapped ions, or photons. They require extreme cold (near absolute zero) to keep quantum coherence.

Quantum computers don't just calculate - they explore the entire landscape of possibility, then find the most probable path.

Final Takeaway:

The world is weirder - and more mathematical - than it looks.

From cats in boxes to the brightness of your screen to the coins in your digital wallet, it's all part of the same universe.

You don't have to understand quantum mechanics to live in it. But if you do - even a little - life starts to look a lot more interesting.

A Closing Thought:

The question isn't, can you change the world. The question is:

What part of the world is waiting for you to begin?

Chapter 11: Into Your Dream Life

You have 24 hours each day.

7 days a week.

That's 168 hours - and what you do with them shapes your entire future.

Living your dream life doesn't require being rich or famous.
It requires being intentional - with your time, your health, your energy, your mindset.

Learn every day - your brain thrives on it.

Your brain has neuroplasticity - the ability to rewire itself through learning.
The more you challenge it, the sharper it stays.
Whether it's learning Korean, playing an instrument, or just reading daily - learning is youth for the mind.

But learning fades fast if you don't use it. Studies show that if you don't apply new knowledge within a few days, most of it disappears. It's like trying to build muscles but never lifting anything. The sooner you use what you learn, the deeper it sticks. So if something sparks your curiosity - a new idea, skill, or insight - test it. Practice it. Teach it. That's how knowledge becomes part of you.

Mistakes aren't failures - they're the best teachers. Every inventor, scientist, and artist knows this. Leonardo da Vinci sketched countless machines that didn't work. Einstein published ideas that later needed correction. Every mistake builds understanding - if you pay attention. The key isn't avoiding mistakes, but learning from them, improving because of them. If you're not making mistakes, you're probably not trying anything new.

A 2012 study from the University of Edinburgh found that lifelong learning slows age-related cognitive decline. [1]

Fun Fact: Taxi drivers in London have significantly larger hippocampus (the brain's memory center) than the average person - because learning thousands of street names actually reshaped their brains. [2]

Eat real food. Move every day. Sleep enough.

Healthy living isn't about extremes - it's about consistency.
Just walking 20–30 minutes a day boosts mood, improves heart health,
and reduces stress.

Sleep? It's not a luxury. It's the control center of your biology.
A single night of sleep deprivation can reduce learning ability by up to
40%. [3]

You don't need perfect meals or workouts - you need daily effort.

Build financial freedom - one decision at a time.

If you're young, use your advantage: time.
Compound interest is the strongest financial force available to you.

And no - you don't need to "beat the market."
Most people don't. In fact, even professional investors don't.

In one famous test, a group of monkeys randomly throwing darts at a
stock list outperformed most fund managers.
In 2013, a five-year-old girl and an orangutan beat seasoned investors by
picking companies at random. [4]

That's why index investing works: it's simple, low-cost, and historically
powerful.

Diversify Like a Scientist.

Your financial future depends on how well you spread your risks. Don't
just save - diversify. Real estate gives stability. Precious metals hedge
against inflation. Crypto offers high-risk, high-reward innovation. Stocks
give long-term growth. Each asset behaves differently - and together,
they create resilience. Diversification isn't just a financial strategy - it
follows the same principles as physics: balance, resilience, and
distributed force.

You're not late.
The best time to plant a tree was 20 years ago.
The second-best time? Now.

Small actions = Big change.

Brush your teeth.
Drink water.
Read 5 pages.
Save $50.
Smile more.
Text a friend.

Every small action, repeated, becomes momentum.
That's compound interest for life - not just finance.

One useful skill? Bifocal vision - seeing both near and far at the same time. It means balancing today's actions with tomorrow's goals. Handle the small things that matter now, but never lose sight of the bigger picture. It's easy to get stuck in either mode - too short-term, and you drift; too long-term, and you never act. Bifocal thinkers build the future one smart step at a time.

Give - and you'll feel richer.

Years ago, I paid for someone's small shop purchase - about $20.
I still remember how good that felt.

Science confirms this: generosity activates the brain's reward centers. It lowers cortisol (stress) and boosts serotonin and dopamine - your natural "feel-good" chemicals. [5]

Giving isn't a subtraction. It's an expansion.
Give what you can - money, time, energy, or your full presence.

Design a life that feels like life.

We've been sold a dream that more money, more stuff, and more screen time equals more happiness. But the data tells a different story.

According to Nobel Prize-winning economist Daniel Kahneman, emotional well-being doesn't improve much after you earn around $75,000 to $100,000 a year. It levels off. More income may help your status - but not your soul. [6]

The same goes for TV. Studies show that heavy television watchers actually report lower life satisfaction and more symptoms of depression. We don't feel alive when we're numbing out. [7]

The most happiness doesn't come from screens or shopping.
It comes from:

Connection
Purpose
Nature
Love

Picture this:
You're lying on a grassy hill. Your partner beside you. The sea in the distance.
Nothing urgent. Just presence.

Studies show that these kinds of experiences - connection, nature, intimacy - are some of the most powerful happiness triggers. According to survey-based research, people often describe sex in outdoor or novel settings, like a quiet hilltop with a sea view, as one of the most joyful, memorable moments of their lives. [8] And it's not just about sex - it's about aliveness. Presence. A sense of being fully in the moment with someone you care about. Real happiness rarely comes from things. It comes from moments like that.

According to Harvard's 75-year happiness study, the quality of your relationships is the single biggest predictor of long-term well-being. [9]

Relationships & Romance: Feel safe - but excited.

In love, one thing matters most: feeling like you can be yourself.
That's when real connection happens - not performance, but presence.

Studies show women are - on average - drawn to men in roles like:

Paramedics
Nurses
Massage Therapists
Firefighters
Pilots

Why?
Because these roles suggest competence, care, and calm under pressure - traits tied to both safety and strength.

Evolutionary psychology shows women are wired to seek both protection and connection. [10]
And excitement matters too - which is why humor, unpredictability, and confidence are also rated highly. [11]

Confidence isn't knowing everything. It's trusting you can figure things out.
That's the trait that moves relationships, businesses, and dreams.

Want wealth? Learn what most never do.

If you want to build lasting financial success, offer something people truly want and need - and position yourself where opportunity exists.

Some of the most consistently high-earning fields - like car dealership owners and sales entrepreneurs - succeed not just by knowing their customers, but by securing smart positions: local demand, limited competition, sometimes even near-monopoly advantages.

Why?
Sales
People
Position
Confidence

And in business - confidence sells.

"If you don't believe in what you're offering, why should anyone else?"
- Dale Carnegie

And if there's one habit that destroys more dreams than anything?
Procrastination.
Waiting, hesitating, overthinking - they kill momentum. Start small. Act today. Consistent action beats perfect plans.

Dream Life Checklist

Want a life you love? Ask yourself daily:

Did I learn something today?
Did I move my body?
Did I invest in my future?
Did I connect with someone I care about?
Did I do one small thing with intention?

It doesn't have to be perfect.
It just has to be yours.

Final Words

Everyone wants their dream life - but few plan for it.
Structure isn't boring. It's freedom.
Planning your week means owning your time - not reacting to it.
In the age of infinite distractions, it's easy to waste hours scrolling, checking, replying. But that's someone else's agenda.
Yours starts with a plan. Stick to it - and you'll be amazed where it takes you.

We try so hard to curate perfect lives - neat calendars, filtered photos, "good vibes only."
But life isn't linear. It's a rollercoaster: highs, lows, loops, and surprise turns.
You don't grow on the flat parts.
You grow in the chaos.

And when things don't go to plan? Don't get angry. I know - easier said than done.
But those unexpected moments? They're not interruptions.
They're psychological enrichment.
Every setback is an emotional weightlift - resistance that builds your inner strength.
You don't just survive it.
You become stronger because of it.

As personal development legend Jim Rohn once said:
"If you don't like where you are, change it. You're not a tree."

And while you're changing, choose wisely who's with you.

Surround yourself with people who elevate you - not distract you.

And when it comes to love, be intentional.

You'll spend most of your life with one person - make sure it's someone you can grow with.

That's one of the most important decisions you'll ever make.

Your dream life isn't wishful thinking - it's a direction.
And the map has been in your hands all along.

Now's the time to stop waiting.
Stop hoping.
Start walking.

The future doesn't belong to the lucky.
It belongs to the intentional.
You've always had the pen.
Now - write the story only you can live.

You Will Forever Regret Not Having Read This Book

Acknowledgments

To my parents - thank you for your endless support, wisdom, and the curiosity you sparked in me from day one.
To my father, especially: perhaps I inherited my perfectionism from you. Together, we've come to see that as both a challenge and a gift.

To my work colleagues and teammates - thank you for the conversations, questions, feedback, and patience during this long creative process. You shaped this more than you know.

To the authors whose books I've read, and to the writers behind the sources and references throughout this work - your insights, research, and ideas helped light the path. This book stands on your shoulders.

To everyone who ever challenged, encouraged, or inspired me - in conversation, friendship, or silence - this book carries pieces of you.

And to the reader:
Thank you for trusting me with your attention.
I wrote this with care, hoping it might offer you clarity, awe, or peace in this complex world we all share.

References & Further Reading

Prologue

1. Hattenstone, S. (2012). Mummy, why do I ask so many questions? The Guardian. Retrieved from https://www.theguardian.com/lifeandstyle/2012/mar/17/children-ask-questions-parents
2. Rothstein, D., & Santana, L. (2011). Make Just One Change: Teach Students to Ask Their Own Questions. Harvard Education Press.

Chapter 2: At Work

1. Statista (2024). Global coffee consumption statistics. [Online]
2. International Coffee Organization. Coffee consumption by region. [Online]
3. National Coffee Association USA. Coffee Belt overview. [Online]
4. Specialty Coffee Association. Coffee roasting and chemistry. [Online]
5. Scientific American. Flavor chemistry and the Maillard reaction in coffee. [Article]
6. Harvard Health & National Institutes of Health (NIH). Caffeine's effect on brain chemistry. [Online]
7. Mayo Clinic. Caffeine: How much is too much? [Online]
8. Dunbar, R. I. M. (Oxford University). The Social Brain Hypothesis. [Academic Theory]
9. Centers for Disease Control and Prevention (CDC). E-cigarette facts and risks. [Online]
10. World Health Organization (WHO). Health effects of vaping. [Online]

Chapter 3: In the City

1. Bradshaw, G. A., et al. (2005). Elephant behavior and trauma. Nature.
2. McComb, K., et al. Elephant social cognition. University of Sussex.
3. Marzluff, J. M., et al. (2010). Crow memory of humans. PNAS, University of Washington.
4. Payne, R., & McVay, S. (1971). Whale song structure. Science.
5. von Frisch, K. (1967). The Dance Language of Bees. University of Würzburg. [Book]

Chapter 5: On the Trail

1. Simard, S. W., et al. (1997). Net carbon transfer between trees. Nature, 388(6642), 579–582.
2. Park, B. J., Tsunetsugu, Y., Kasetani, T., et al. (2010). The physiological effects of Shinrin-yoku (forest bathing) on stress reduction: Evidence from field experiments. Environmental Health and Preventive Medicine, 15(1), 18–26.

Chapter 6: With Others

1. Dunbar, R. I. M. The Social Brain Hypothesis. [Academic Theory]
2. Gollwitzer, P. M. (1999). Implementation Intentions. American Psychologist.
3. Carmody, D., & Lewis, P. A. (2006). Brain activation to one's own name. [Study]
4. Purves, D., et al. Neuroscience (6th ed.). [Textbook]
5. Carnegie, D. How to Win Friends and Influence People. [Book]
6. Rizzolatti, G., & Craighero, L. (2004). Mirror neurons. Annual Review of Neuroscience.

Chapter 7: Inside the Body

1. Carr, A. C., et al. (2013). Vitamin C improves mood and vitality. [Study]
2. Draganski, B., et al. (2006). Neuroplasticity and grey matter. NeuroImage, 31(2), 710–721.
3. Oppezzo, M., & Schwartz, D. L. (2014). Walking boosts creativity. Journal of Experimental Psychology.
4. Cryan, J. F., & Dinan, T. G. (2012). Gut microbiota and behavior. Nature Reviews Neuroscience
5. Bhogale, D., et al. (2022). Recent Synergy of Nanodiamonds: Role in Brain-Targeted Drug Delivery for the Management of Neurological Disorders. Molecular Neurobiology
6. Margulis, L. (1970). Origin of Eukaryotic Cells. Yale University Press.
7. Gómez-Pinilla, F. (2008). Brain foods: the effects of nutrients on brain function. Nature Reviews Neuroscience. PLOS ONE (2013): Meta-analysis of omega-3 fatty acids and cognitive function
8. Bischoff-Ferrari HA, Vollenweider D, Dawson-Hughes B, et al. Individual and additive effects of vitamin D, omega-3 and exercise on

DNA methylation clocks of biological aging in older adults:
DO-HEALTH trial. Nature Aging. 2024; PMID: 39900648

Chapter 8: Inside the Mind

1. Kahneman, D. (2011). Thinking, Fast and Slow. [Book]
2. Bargh, J. A., & Morsella, E. (2008). The unconscious mind. Perspectives on Psychological Science, 3(1), 73–79.
3. Mayer, E. A. (2011). Gut-brain communication. Nature Reviews Neuroscience.
4. Dunn, B. D., et al. (2010). Interoception and decision-making. Journal of Experimental Psychology.
5. Raichle, M. E., & Gusnard, D. A. (2002). Brain energy use. PNAS, 99(16), 10237–10239.
6. Gilbert, D. T. (2006). Stumbling on Happiness. [Book]
7. Wilson, T. D., et al. (2014). The disengaged mind. Science, 345(6192), 75–77.
8. Andrews, S., et al. (2015). Smartphone use vs. estimates. PLOS ONE, 10(10), e0139004.
9. Bawden, D., & Robinson, L. (2020). Information overload. Oxford Encyclopedia of Political Decision Making.
10. Steel, P. (2007). Procrastination meta-analysis. Psychological Bulletin, 133(1), 65–94.
11. Ariely, D., & Wertenbroch, K. (2002). Precommitment and procrastination. Psychological Science, 13(3), 219–224.
12. Claxton, G. (1997). Hare Brain, Tortoise Mind. [Book]
13. Beaty, R. E., et al. (2016). Default mode network and creativity. NeuroImage, 142, 94–103.

Chapter 9: Under Influence

1. Ethnologue. (2023). Global language statistics. [Online] https://www.ethnologue.com
2. Iacoboni, M. (2009). Mirroring People: The New Science of How We Connect with Others. [Book]
3. Schultz, W. (1998). Dopamine reward signals. Journal of Neurophysiology, 80(1), 1–27.

4. Langer, E., Blank, A., & Chanowitz, B. (1978). The mindlessness of ostensibly thoughtful action: The role of "placebic" information in interpersonal interaction. Journal of Personality and Social Psychology.

5. Libet, B. (1985). Unconscious cerebral initiative and the role of conscious will in voluntary action. Behavioral and Brain Sciences.

6. Harris, J. R. (1995). Group socialization theory. Psychological Review, 102(3), 458–489.

7. Boroditsky, L. (2011). How language shapes thought. Scientific American, 304(2), 62–65.

8. Tversky, A., & Kahneman, D. (1973). Availability heuristic. Cognitive Psychology, 5(2), 207–232.

Chapter 10: The Bigger Picture

1. Centola, D., Becker, J., Brackbill, D., & Baronchelli, A. (2018). Experimental evidence for tipping points in social convention. Science, 360(6393), 1116–1119.

2. Fowler, J. H., & Christakis, N. A. (2010). Cooperative behavior cascades in human social networks. PNAS, 107(12), 5334–5338.

Chapter 11: Into Your Dream Life

1. Gow, A. J., et al. (2012). Cognitive ability and education: Lifelong learning slows age-related cognitive decline. University of Edinburgh Study.

2. Woollett, K., & Maguire, E. A. (2011). Acquiring 'the Knowledge' of London's layout drives structural brain changes. Current Biology, 21(24), 2109–2114.

3. Walker, M. P. (2007). The role of sleep in memory and learning. Scientific American, 18(5), 22–27.

4. BBC News. (2013). Orangutan and child beat professionals in stock-picking challenge. BBC News [Online].

5. Moll, J., et al. (2006). Human fronto–mesolimbic networks guide decisions about charitable donation. PNAS, 103(42), 15623–15628.

6. Kahneman, D., & Deaton, A. (2010). High income improves evaluation of life but not emotional well-being. Proceedings of the National Academy of Sciences (PNAS).

7. Csikszentmihalyi, M., & Kubey, R. (2002). Television addiction is no mere metaphor. Scientific American.

8. Muise, A., Schimmack, U., & Impett, E. A. (2015). Sexual frequency and happiness. Social Psychological and Personality Science.
9. Waldinger, R. J., & Schulz, M. S. (2010). The Harvard Study of Adult Development. Harvard University.
10. Buss, D. M., & Schmitt, D. P. (1993). Sexual Strategies Theory: An evolutionary perspective on human mating. Psychological Review, 100(2), 204–232.
11. Li, N. P., Griskevicius, V., et al. (2002). Preferences in human mate selection: Humor and risk-taking. Journal of Personality and Social Psychology, 82(6), 947–955.

About the Author

Flobse Wild is a globally experienced business professional with a background in the automotive, construction, and semiconductor industries. Having lived in five different countries, he combines real-world insight with a passion for learning, curiosity, and practical wisdom.

He is deeply interested in science, psychology, language, and how the world works. Flobse loves reading, sharing knowledge, and helping others grow - and his writing reflects that mission with clarity, depth, and heart.

This is his second book. His first, Heartbroken - Man, I Feel You, was a deeply personal response to rejection and heartbreak. In it, he poured his heart out to help other men navigate emotional pain - a book born from raw experience and a desire to support those who often suffer in silence.

In contrast, The Most Important Book You Will Ever Read About Life has been a longer, more deliberate journey. Built over time, it's his ambitious attempt to connect everything - from atoms to meaning - into one powerful, clear, and accessible guide to understanding the world.

He currently resides in Switzerland.

In case of questions, remarks, or media requests, please visit:

www.flobsewild.com

www.youwillforeverregret.com

Or email us at: contact@flobsewild.com

Printed in Dunstable, United Kingdom